Exceptional Children in Focus

James S. Payne
James M. Kauffman
Gweneth B. Brown
Richard M. DeMott

University of Virginia

Charles E. Merrill Publishing Company
A Bell & Howell Company
Columbus, Ohio

To Norris G. Haring
advisor, teacher, friend, scholar, writer . . .
used car salesman

Published by
Charles E. Merrill Publishing Co.
A Bell & Howell Co.
Columbus, Ohio

International Standard Book Number: 0-675-08828-3

Library of Congress Catalog Card Number: 73-93273

1   2   3   4   5   6   7   8   9   10 — 78   77   76   75   74

Printed in the United States of America

Preface

We hope that this book will provide you with a readable, compact, stimulating overview of the field of exceptional children. Currently survey texts supply you with a more than adequate exposure to exceptionalities on an academic and cognitive level. These texts are packed with many definitions, prevalence and incidence data, and astonishing facts showing that the retarded are slow thinkers, that learning disabled children have academic problems in school, that visually impaired students have difficulty seeing, that emotionally disturbed children misbehave, and that the hearing impaired cannot hear very well. The text you are about to read is concerned with the feelings and ideas engendered by association with exceptional children as well as the most basic facts. We view exceptional children as people, not merely as statistics.

In our first chapter, we demonstrate that people can make simple things confusing and easy things difficult. We've just tried to make things simple and easy. For each area of exceptionality we have used anecdotes to illustrate that the retarded can learn, that emotionally disturbed kids are not completely crazy, that most blind people can actually see a little bit, that learning disabled kids are brighter than they appear, that the gifted are not just intelligent, and that the hard of hearing can understand. Our anecdotes are followed by basic information: definition, prevalence, and etiology. The basic information is followed by discussion of a fundamental concept or current issue. At the end of each chapter we have provided questions for you to ponder. These questions are designed to help you integrate the information, concepts, and issues.

We are grateful to Dr. C. Lee Woods for his editorial assistance on Chapter 5. Dr. Virgil S. Ward gave us helpful comments on Chapter 8. Jeanne L. Sauter provided editorial assistance on Chapter 4. Linda Wilberger receives our gratitude for her tireless and patient typing and retyping of the manuscript.

Contents

one

Introduction to Exceptionality

People who work with exceptional children all too often convey the impression that life is always serious and tragic. Stressing the sorrows which arise in handicapped children, these people tend to overlook the joys and rewards that abound in the field of special education. Moreover, professors in teacher training institutions so often preoccupy themselves with statistical data that they neglect to give students a "feel" for who exceptional children really are and what it is like to work with them. Thus, prospective teachers may get the erroneous impression that working in special education will be dry, tedious, or worst of all, an experience full of sadness.

Quite to the contrary, we have found working with exceptional children exciting, engaging, and a largely happy occupation. Despite occasional moments of sorrow, there is a world of joy and delightful experience. Often a sense of humor helps both student and teacher to face each new day. When working with exceptional children one's perspective becomes very important. We can mourn because a rosebush has thorns or rejoice because a thornbush has roses. Teachers and students who cannot see the joy and humor present in their struggles will soon find the thorns draining their enthusiasm and strength to endure the difficult periods.

The other day the little four-year-old girl from next door came over and watched me rake leaves. For over thirty minutes she watched and then, out of the blue, said, "My daddy has a glass eye." Well, how do you respond to that? Since I didn't know what to say or do, I just kept on raking the leaves and nonchalantly said, "Oh." She continued, "Yeah, he really does, but I don't understand it. He can't see any better with it in than he can with it out."

Most people would agree that there's humor in the innocence of that four-year-old's statement. It's funny to me, it's probably funny to you, and it was certainly funny to my one-eyed neighbor. Thank goodness we can occasionally share a laugh about a circumstance which involves an unfortunate condition.

After undertaking the writing of this book, we looked up one day from some of our professional journals full of confusing definitions, conflicting results, and elaborate theories. We suddenly realized we had fallen into the same trap as had many others in attempting to teach students about exceptional children. We had blindly missed the essence of our field. Our preoccupation with academic analysis had distracted us from viewing the emotional side of our work. We had forgotten the joy of watching as a crippled child took his first steps, as a retarded child finally learned to write his name, and as an emotionally disturbed child brought his temper under control. We had even forgotten about the disappointment we experienced when a retarded child returned from vacation having lost all that he had worked so hard to learn, the agony we felt in holding down a self-destructive, emotionally disturbed child, and the anxiety that shook us as we told desperate parents about the complete lack of local services for their child.

If we, as professionals in special education, don't project the joys as well as the pains of working with exceptional people, we are not projecting reality. If students enroll in an introductory course about exceptional children and they learn only how many times a mongoloid rocks during lunchtime, the frequency of thumbsucks of a severely retarded child, the number of head-bangs exhibited before extinction by an emotionally disturbed child, the six definitions of the blind — then it is no wonder that handicapped individuals

are thought to be weird. And it is no wonder that the people working with handicapped children are thought to be a little crazy too.

Many professors, in trying to help students grasp essential
but often confusing information, forget to communicate the emotionally appealing aspects of special education. In their zeal, these
professors also frequently entangle students in complicated details
of very simple concepts. Consider the following brief lecture on the
exogenous-endogenous concept.

Every introductory text about exceptional children will
mention the terms "exogenous" and "endogenous." Most of
these survey texts mention that the terms are used differently
by different authorities in the field, but go on to say that
usually exogenous is a term referring to the causes of mental
retardation which originate outside or external to the body
and which are synonymous with pathological causes. Endogenous usually refers to causes of mental retardation that originate within the body or central nervous system and are
synonymous with nonpathological causes or cultural-familial
mental retardation. Examples of exogenous causes of mental
retardation include chromosomal anomalies, metabolic disorders, blood type incompatability, hypoxia (anoxia), prematurity of birth, etc. — all of which, at first glance, seem to
be causes occurring inside rather than outside of the body. The
majority of endogenous, or cultural familial cases of mental
retardation are caused by a combination of biological and environmental factors. Of course, the big emphasis should be on
the environment which, it seems to me, is on the outside of the
body rather than on the inside. Most dictionaries define the
terms as they relate to plants. Large and more expensive dictionaries do define exogenous as "having its origin external"
while endogenous refers to "originating within." It seems that
exogenous means outside, but when it is related to causes of
mental retardation it means inside, and endogenous means
inside, but when it is related to mental retardation it means
outside.

Now, the simple truth about these two terms is this. When
someone uses the term "endogenous," consider child-rearing practices, lack of educational opportunity, and inheritance as possible
factors contributing to the retardation. When someone uses the
term "exogenous," consider genetic abnormalities, physical trauma,

disease, prematurity, and metabolic disorders as possible factors contributing to the retardation.

Of course, once you finish your introductory course you probably will never hear the terms used again. While few professors who teach introductory courses overlook the opportunity to test students on the concept, in all of our years working in the field of special education we have never heard a teacher, counselor, principal, parent, or retarded child utter either "exogenous" or "endogenous." In fact, the recent *Manual on Terminology and Classification in Mental Retardation* (Grossman, 1973) lists them as obsolete.

Students are confounded in many ways. The following illustrates how another special education professor chose to test his class.

Students taking an introductory course in special education had just completed a class in tests and measurements and understood the normal curve better than their special education professor. It had been some time since the professor had thoroughly studied statistical distributions and, unfortunately, he was oblivious to the fact that his students had studied the curve very recently. With all the erudition that he could muster, the professor explained, "As you will observe, the normal curve is symmetrical, like a bell. Indeed, I'm sure you will find that this distribution is usually called the 'bell-shaped' curve."

Much sooner than the students would have preferred, final exam time rolled around. Lo and behold, not only was their professor a daring and dramatic lecturer, but he also had a talent for writing confusing test questions! One on the normal curve went as follows:

The normal curve is: (choose the *best* answer)

    a.   symmetrical
    b.   bell-shaped
    c.   doesn't really matter
    d.   who cares anyway

Most good students resist their impulse to circle *d* and fluctuate between *a* and *b*. The students in this class, however, had trouble deciding on their answer. Having just completed their tests and measurement course, they knew immediately that the correct answer *must* be *a* — symmetrical. But that was not the answer that the professor liked. "It's quite clear," he stated, "the answer is *b* because bells are symmetrical which includes *a*. Since there are many symmetrical things that are not bell-shaped, by the process of elimination *b* is the best answer." After hearing this explanation, most of the students groaned, and some young rebels stormed out of the room. But no manner of protest or persuasion moved the steadfast professor. He loved his question and he loved his answer. He was even heard mumbling to himself, "I love it! I love it! I can tell the bright students from the not so bright just by this one question. The poor students think I'm just throwing them a curve, yuk, yuk, yuk!"

Not long after the course ended, a group of admiring students anonymously presented the professor with a token of their appreciation. Hanging on his office door one morning were three bells — a trapezoidal cowbell, a round sleigh bell, and a square bell. The thank you note which was attached to the bells read, "Take these bells and. . . ."

Our message is simple: Special education is exciting and vibrantly alive. Rather than permitting dry academic commentary, nit-picking detail, and only sorrowful emotional experiences to dominate introductory approaches to special education, basic courses should impart a flavor of the personal joy of dealing with the exceptional child.

With this idea as our premise, we have pushed aside traditional academic format and customary formalities in an attempt to provide you with a light, enjoyable reading experience. You needn't take copious notes or scrutinize the print; just sit back, gather a little basic information and share with us the simple joys of working with exceptional children.

two

Learning Disability

Anna was in the sixth grade. She was a good student in most respects. She tried hard and did acceptable work in most areas. She was easy to get along with and related well to her peers. She just couldn't spell.

Most sixth-grade classes love art projects and mine was no exception. I had acquired a kiln and some clay discarded by another school in the district, and we were having a really great time making all kinds of things. Anna brought me a beautiful slab pot that she had just finished. It was about two inches high and six inches in diameter, and I commented on its nice form and proportion in addition to the quality of construction. Obviously elated, Anna said that she was going to label her bowl so that everyone would know what is was (she didn't like having it called a "pot") and hurried off to do the job. About twenty minutes later she was back with her bowl. In perfectly formed, two-inch letters she had written on the side of her treasure, BOWEL.

Billy was a sixth-grader who could spell. He could also read and do arithmetic just fine. But often all was not well with the way he heard things and the things that he said. Technically, one might say he had trouble with the auditory-vocal channel. He had special difficulty in understanding and using oral language. Now, when children do not seem to understand what they are told, teachers become irritated. And when children say things that seemingly make no sense, teachers start to think the children are weird. Under these circumstances, the children often try to cover up the problem with diversionary tactics. Two of Billy's diversionary tactics were talking in a very high-pitched, thin little voice and making simulated "pass gas" noises. So it is really no wonder that Billy ended up in my class for children with special learning problems.

Soon after he came into my class, Billy had a birthday. We had a little celebration in class, during which I asked Billy what gifts, if any, he was getting at home. He asked me what I meant, and I said, "I mean what presents are you getting — what are your mom and dad giving you for your birthday?"

"Oh," he answered, "I think a Chesterdrors."

"A Chesterdrors?" I asked.

"Yeah."

Not wanting to appear dumb, I thought about it for a while. But I couldn't for the life of me figure out what he was talking about.

"Billy, what is a Chesterdrors?"

"Just a Chesterdrors, that's all."

"Well, what does it look like?"

I could see I was going to come out of this one looking dumb, but I had to go all the way now.

"I dunno, just like a Chesterdrors."

"How big is it, I mean how tall?"

"Oh, about this high, I guess," holding his hand about the height of his head.

"What do you do with it — what do you use it for?"

"Just to put clothes and stuff in."

"You mean a chest of drawers?"

"Yeah, I *said* a Chesterdrors!"

I explained to Billy that chest of drawers is three words. We wrote them and talked about them. By the time he went home,

I thought he understood — he was saying the three words distinctly.

The next day I asked Billy what he had gotten for his birthday.

"Just a Chesterdrors," he said.

Arithmetic was Dick's nemesis. He hated it with such a passion that he would often end up talking to himself while working on an assignment, muttering threats half at me and half at the work, and fantasizing what the world would be like if he were in control of such drudgery and incomprehensible nonsense.

"If I were a judge," he said, "I would sentence people to five years at hard arithmetic."

"Arithmetic is a part of life," I said, "like eating and sleeping."

"Yeah, and like a cancer growing inside you, too. If I were God, I'd start all over again and make the world without numbers this time."

For two years Dick fought his enemy, but only at my insistence. Now he was nearly fourteen and would soon be leaving my special class for a regular junior high class. As a parting gesture of goodwill and confidence I thought I'd give him a week's reprieve — a week free from that intolerable "garbage" he had to work on every day. That ought to convince him that the world isn't all bad and that maybe one can even have a little paradise on earth.

But I had not kept up with the transformation that had taken place.

"You can't do this to me," he pleaded. "Not now after all these years. It just isn't fair. I just wouldn't feel right without a little arithmetic. Besides, I kind of like it. It's part of life — like eating and sleeping."

Definition

In 1968 the National Advisory Committee on Handicapped Children of the U.S. Office of Education proposed the following definition of learning disabilities:

Children with special (specific) learning disabilities exhibit a disorder in one or more of the basic psychological processes involved in understanding or in using spoken or written language. These may be manifested in disorders of listening, thinking, talking, reading, writing, spelling, or arithmetic. They include conditions which have been referred to as perceptual handicaps, brain injury, minimal brain dysfunction, dyslexia, developmental aphasia, etc. They *do not* include learning problems which are due primarily to visual, hearing, or motor handicaps, to mental retardation, emotional disturbance, or to environmental disadvantage (p. 14).

Many other definitions have been written since learning disabilities became an identifiable area of special education in the early 1960s. Some of them have emphasized neurological dysfunction or central processing deficits, while others have highlighted the behavioral aspects involved. All recognize that learning disabilities may vary along a continuum from mild to severe.

In essence, children with learning disabilities have been defined by exclusion — they are not emotionally disturbed, culturally disadvantaged, retarded, visibly crippled (although the term "invisibly crippled" has been used), or deaf or blind — they just do not learn some specific, basic developmental and academic tasks as most children do. And nobody knows for sure why.

Because learning disabilities is a relatively new area of study, service, and research, definitions are still in an experimental, developmental stage. As the field develops, it is possible that learning disabilities may be redefined in more narrow terms to include fewer children with more specific characteristics. It is also possible that learning disabilities may become a generic term for learning problems of all kinds, regardless of the suspected etiology and related disabilities.

Prevalence

For 1971–72 the U.S. Office of Education used a prevalance estimate of 1 per cent for children with specific learning disabilities. To many knowledgeable persons in the field this seems to be a very conservative estimate; a more realistic figure may be 3–7 per cent depending upon the definition used and the severity of the disorders included. Before a truly realistic estimate of prevalance can be determined, issues of definition must be resolved.

Etiology

As mentioned previously, learning disabilities have traditionally been defined by exclusion. Consequently, it has been denied that children become learning disabled because of mental retardation, emotional disturbance, visual or auditory impairment, crippling conditions, or environmental disadvantage (lack of appropriate stimulation or opportunity to learn). What is left? As the argument goes, if the child is not learning and his lack of achievement cannot be explained in any other way, there must be something wrong in his head — he must be brain damaged.

Now, as will be mentioned in the discussion of the etiologies of other exceptionalities, brain damage can result from a very large number of factors. But knowing that brains *can* be injured by many factors does not prove that a given child's brain *has* been injured. It is also extremely difficult to provide conclusive evidence that a child's learning disability is the direct *result* of brain injury, even if it is *known* that his brain has been damaged. Consequently, it is safe to say only that brain injury is a suspected etiological factor in many cases of learning disability.

By most definitions, seriously emotionally disturbed children are excluded from the learning disabled population. There is little doubt that emotional factors are involved in learning disabilities, however. Mildly emotionally disturbed and learning disabled children do exhibit many similar characteristics. But it is not clear whether emotional disturbance is an etiological factor in or a consequence of a learning disability.

There is a third possible etiological factor in learning disabilities which special educators are only now beginning to face squarely—inadequate teaching (Bruner, 1971; Cohen, 1971). While it would be ridiculous to suggest that *all* learning disabled children have been poorly taught, it seems likely that in a significant number of cases the problem is as much one of providing appropriate instruction as of finding the child's disability. This line of thought places a lot of responsibility on the teacher, but that is where it should be. If a child is not learning, it can only be concluded that his teacher has not found an effective way of teaching him. The malady may be as much in the teacher's lack of instructional prowess as in the child's lack of ability to perform.

Learning Disabled or Learning Dyslabeled?

Given the ambiguities and controversy surrounding the definition of learning disabilities, it is not surprising that there are arguments about what the children in question should be called. Concern for the label to be attached to those who have only recently been recognized as a distinct group of handicapped individuals is heightened by the realization that other special education labels seem to have a deleterious effect on children. It is no secret that "retarded" can be a bad name, and it does not take a genius to recognize that "emotionally disturbed," "autistic," "stutterer," "crippled," "hyperactive," or any other special term used to describe a handicapped individual can likewise become an epithet designed to hurt or degrade the person. Many of the people who were instrumental in developing the "new" field of learning disabilities in the 1960s were also determined to avoid stigmatizing still another group of children. In a frantic effort to foil the pernicious influence of labels known to carry negative connotations, these people thought up a wide variety of new ones, all of them used at some time or other to refer to essentially the same type of child or condition:

Atypical Child	Minimal Cerebral Dysfunction
Brain Injured	Organic Brain Syndrome
Choreiform Child	Performance Deviation
Developmental Aphasia	Performance Disabled
Developmentally Imbalanced	Performance Handicapped
Driven Child	Problem Learner
Dyslexia	Problem Reader
Dyssynchronous Child	Psycholinguistic Disability
Educationally Handicapped	Psychoneurological Disorder
Educationally Maladjusted	Psychoneurological Learning
Hyperactive Behavior Disorder	Disability
Hyperkinetic Child	Reading Disability
Interjacent Child	Remedial Education Case
Invisibly Crippled Child	Special Learning Disability
Language Disordered	Specific Learning Disability
Learning Disabled	Strauss Syndrome
Learning Impaired	Underachiever
Minimal Brain Dysfunction	

Predictably, as soon as people found out what these labels really meant the names became noxious. Of course, what's derogatory in a name is the social role or quality or deviancy or conformity it suggests. In our society the imagery conjured up by *any* label for a handicapping condition tends to be stigmatizing, not because of the label itself, but because of our archaic attitudes toward handicaps. The stigma of being exceptional will not go away, no matter what the label, until a handicap is no longer the reason for pity, mourning, disgust, humor, segregation, or reverence. When we can laugh, cry, teach, learn, struggle, and enjoy life with handicapped people as we do with other individuals who share our human limitations, there will be no pain in labels.

But stigma is not the only problem with labeling. We need to classify people in order to avoid total confusion and miscommunication. The real issues in labeling are: "Labeled according to what criteria?" "Labeled by whom?" and "Labeled for what purpose?" When labels are based on objective and relevant criteria, are applied by responsible professionals, and are used to communicate essential information about an individual, they can even be helpful to the individuals involved.

There are numerous factors which are known to influence how a child is perceived and categorized including (a) the social role and cultural context of children's behavior, (b) the fads and predispositions of labelers, (c) the legislation and legal rules regarding exceptional children, and (d) the awareness or unawareness of environmental cues for children's behavior on the part of diagnosticians. Some of these factors inevitably contribute to "dyslabelia."

Social and cultural contexts. These vary from location to location and change over time. In our country, attitudes toward the behavior of children in school have changed dramatically over the last century. Gnagey (1969) reports that S. L. Pressey found a list of misbehaviors and recommended punishments published in North Carolina in 1848. Among them were:

Playing cards at school (10 lashes)

Swearing at school (8 lashes)

Drinking liquor at school (8 lashes)

Telling lies (7 lashes)

Boys and girls playing together (4 lashes)

Quarreling (4 lashes)

Wearing long fingernails (2 lashes)

Blotting one's copybook (2 lashes)

Neglecting to bow when going home (2 lashes)

Today, many Americans would be more likely to recommend lashes for wearing long hair or for a student's *insistence* on bowing when going home. The important thing to remember is that whether or not a child is considered disturbed, retarded, learning disabled, speech handicapped, gifted, and so forth, depends to a significant degree on when, where, and with whom he lives and works; i.e., on the demands and expectations of his environment. A case in point is that most mildly retarded children are not considered retarded until they enter school and are not thought of as retarded by most people after they leave the school environment.

Fads and predispositions. Labels for exceptional children become fashionable and go out of style as do clothes and furniture. People who label children — physicians, psychologists, educators — are influenced by "in" terms. A child may receive a certain label because it "sounds right" or because it is more acceptable to his parents than another term that seems to be more denigrating. White and Charry (1966) studied approximately 3,000 referrals to school psychologists. They found a significant relationship between the child's socioeconomic level and IQ and the label he was given. Children low in IQ and socioeconomic level more often were labeled "culturally disadvantaged" or "educationally inadequate," while children high in IQ and socioeconomic level were more often labeled "brain injured" or "emotionally disturbed." It seemed clear to these investigators that the labelers had definite biases or expectations that influenced how they chose to interpret and label children's behavior.

Legislation and legal rules. It is not a complete distortion of reality to say that legislation and school codes sometimes "make" exceptional children. It is obvious to most of us which children need help, but what to call them is a problem. Now, if a state legislature decides that money and services will be available for "educationally handicapped" children, then "educationally handicapped" children will be identified and served in the schools of that state, regardless of the fact that in another state they would be labeled "learning disabled," "maladjusted," or "Type 600." For example, for a number of years the state of Illinois decided that "maladjusted children . . . means children between the ages of 5 and 21 years who, because of social or emotional problems, are unable to make constructive use of their school experience and require the provisions of special services designed to promote their educational growth and development" (The School Code of Illinois, 14-1, par. 2). Children who in most states would be considered "learning disabled" were considered, in Illinois, to be "maladjusted" because "social problems" was interpreted as "serious educational maladjustment resulting from extreme discrepancy between ability and school achievement associated with such factors as perceptual impairment, severe learning disorders, and neurological disorders" (Article VII, Rule 7.01b). One is tempted to speculate that if funds were provided for "sinful" children, wickedness would abound among our youngsters.

Environmental cues. No one likes to take the rap for children's educational deficiencies — not parents, and certainly not teachers who are always tempted to look outside the classroom for the reasons for the child's lack of success. The mind, the intelligence, the culture, the emotions, the family, the brain — certainly, somehow, somewhere, teachers hope to find the locus of the problem and avoid having the buck stop with them. How often have children been labeled mentally retarded, learning disabled, or emotionally disturbed primarily because the teacher did not recognize his own ineptitude? It is clear that many times teachers inadvertently reinforce the very behavior they want to stop (cf. Stainback, Payne, Stainback and Payne, 1973; Wallace and Kauffman, 1973) or simply do not know how to teach effectively (cf. Becker, 1971).

In conclusion, we want to emphasize the point that labels themselves do not add any information to our store of knowledge, offer any explanation of what is observed, or provide new insights. Labels are only succinct ways of communicating a concept or set of expectations. There is danger in thinking that once a problem is classified or labeled a solution has been found and appropriate intervention will follow automatically. There is also danger in using labels as explanations for behavior, a type of circular reasoning known as reification.

"Why isn't this child, who appears to be of normal intelligence, learning to read?"

"Well, because he has a learning disability."

"But, how do you know that he is learning disabled?"

"Because he appears to have normal intelligence but he isn't learning to read."

The danger in reification or in labeling for its own sake is that sloppy thinking will prevent children from being helped. Exceptional children have suffered too many indignities and waited too long for effective education for us to play games with their names.

Ponder These

1

   You are a teacher in a school district that provides special education services *only* for the "mentally retarded." The services for "retarded" children are excellent and tailored to the needs of individual children regardless of their IQs. You have a child in your class who obviously needs special education services but who does *not* appear to be mentally retarded. Argue the pros and cons of having the child labeled "mentally retarded" so that he can receive a more appropriate education rather than languish in his regular class.

2

   What are the advantages and disadvantages of attributing a child's learning problems to brain damage or brain dysfunction in the absence of unequivocal medical evidence of damage to his brain?

3

When teaching the l _ _ _ _ _ _ _ d _ _ _ _ _ _ _
Behavior is often mislabeled
When a kid doesn't learn
To his b _ _ _ n people turn
And that's why we say he's dys _ _ _ _ _ _ _.

References

Becker, W. C. (Ed.) *An empirical basis for change in education.* Chicago: Science Research Associates, 1971.

Bruner, E. C. Teaching disorders. In B. Bateman (Ed.), *Learning disorders,* Vol. 4. Seattle, Wash.: Special Child, 1971. Pp. 17–44.

Cohen, S. A. Dyspedagogia as a cause of reading retardation. In B. Bateman (Ed.), *Learning disorders,* Vol. 4. Seattle, Wash.: Special Child, 1971. Pp. 269–91.

Gnagey, W. J. *The psychology of discipline in the classroom.* New York: Macmillan, 1968.

National Advisory Committee on Handicapped Children. *First Annual Report.* Washington, D.C.: U.S. Office of Education, 1968.

Stainback, W., J. S. Payne, S. Stainback, and R. A. Payne. *Establishing a token economy in the classroom.* Columbus, Ohio: Charles E. Merrill, 1973.

Wallace, G. and J. M. Kauffman. *Teaching children with learning problems.* Columbus, Ohio: Charles E. Merrill, 1973.

White, M. A. and J. Charry (Eds.) *School disorder, intelligence, and social class.* New York: Teachers College Press, 1966.

three

Emotional Disturbance

I was aware, of course, that emotionally disturbed children sometimes have wild fantasies, but I was not prepared for Wanda. Wanda was eleven years old when I met her. She had a tested IQ of about 160, but it didn't do her much good except, perhaps, to enrich her fantasy life. I was never able to find a topic of conversation, an area of the curriculum, a place, or a time that was free of her bizarre imaginings. She had fantasies about jeans — she "wore" special forty-pocket and hundred-pocket jeans with zippers in the front and drew stylized pictures of them. She had fantasies about the president and the governor and crucifixes and *The Pit and the Pendulum*, doctors, nurses, swimming pools, toilets, injections, physical examinations, Project Mercury (this was in 1962), moles (she had one on her arm that was a microphone into which she talked and one on her leg that was a thermostat controlling her body temperature) . . . there was no end.

When she engaged in her fantasies, Wanda got a peculiar, fixed grin on her face, her eyes became glazed, she giggled, and she talked (often apparently to herself) in a high-pitched, squeaky voice. Frequently, she drew pictures with captions representing the fantasied object and activities. Sometimes she engaged in other bizarre behaviors, such as flattening herself on the floor or wall, kissing it, caressing it, and talking to it. It was impossible to teach Wanda or to have a rational conversation with her while she was fantasizing, and she was "in" fantasy most of the time. It was impossible to predict when, during times of lucidity and reality-oriented behavior, she would suddenly enter her fantasy world again.

Mostly, Wanda had fantasies about buildings. She carried on conversations with them, and they took on human characteristics. Certain parts of buildings — doors, floors, windows, chimneys, porches, and the like—sometimes became separate entities with lives of their own. At other times, these parts of buildings were body parts to be physically examined, injected, or manipulated. Custodians and engineers were, to Wanda, "building doctors." "Dr. Brady just sprayed some white stuff in Bonnie's ass" could be translated to mean that the chief building engineer had just sprayed some lubricant in the door locks in the residence hall.

Wanda had some very special building acquaintances: Elmer (the school building), the governor's mansion (it actually had a name — Cedar Crest), capitol buildings (it didn't really matter which one — they were all prized for their domes), certain churches (those with more than one steeple were special), and the White House (even though it had a peculiar and irreverent habit of "passing gas from under the South Portico"). Wanda also had some favorite building parts. A dome or cupola was, in her terms, a "Beulah Murphy." And a "Beulah Murphy" was a breast. A church steeple represented a penis. Buildings always cried from their windows and talked out of their doors.

I worked with Wanda as a teacher in an institutional school for two years. By the time she was thirteen, she had made some academic progress and seemed to have her fantasy under a little better control, but her imagination still ran very wild.

Six years later, when she was nineteen, I saw her again. I had, meanwhile, moved to another state and had not seen her for at least three years. She was, I had heard, now living in a boarding home and working as a busboy in the restaurant in the motel where I happened to be staying while attending a conference. Much to my dismay, I learned that the windows from the old governor's mansion (a new mansion had been built) were used in the construction of the restaurant and the old mansion's "Beulah Murphy" had been transplanted to the top of the motel.

When I met Wanda in the restaurant she recognized me almost immediately and we talked for a few minutes about how things were going with her — quite well, apparently.

Then suddenly she said, "You know, I don't have those old fantasies about buildings any more. Only, now these dishes talk to me."

Rodney's personal care habits were atrocious. He seemed to attract dirt, grease, and filth. His vocabulary was also foul, and he was generally just plain obnoxious. Not always, though — for he could be very likeable. However, most of the time he found ways of making people want to get away from him as fast as possible and stay away for as long as possible. It is hard to imagine a more repulsive twelve-year-old, and it is no wonder that he found his way into the psychiatric hospital where I was teaching.

In school, the work Rodney handed in reflected his personality. He picked his nose until it bled and wiped the blood and mucus on his papers. He picked his ears and wiped the wax on his papers. He picked his acne and wiped the blood and pus on his papers. He spit on his papers and smeared the saliva over his answers to try to erase them. When he did use an eraser, he made holes. He wrote answers at the wrong place and then circled them and drew arrows, often to another wrong place. He wrote four-lettered words and drew lewd pictures and swastikas on his papers. He punched holes in his papers, tore them, wadded them, taped them together, ripped them apart again, and retaped them. All the while, he muttered curses — he couldn't do the damned work because it was too babyish or too hard or too stupid or too crazy and "what kind of a stupid goddamned bastard was I to give him such crap?"

Rodney made himself the bane of everyone's existence. He teased and bullied smaller children unmercifully. He baited teachers and threatened other adults. Cleanliness and pleasantness seemed completely foreign to him. He referred to his former teacher most often as "f _ _ _ stick."

My first confrontation with Rodney was the first minute of the first day I tried to teach him. He sauntered into the classroom, took one look at me, and said, "If you're going to be in here, then I'm getting the hell out!" In an instant, he was out the door, around the corner, up two flights of stairs, and out of the building. It did not take me long to realize that I had to go after him and bring him back, even if it meant dragging him. I caught up with him about twenty feet outside the building. I fully expected that we would have a physical struggle and I would end up dragging him back to the classroom. Instead, when I reached out to grab him he stopped, looked at me for a moment, and said, "Well, hell! I guess I might as well go back." He got back to the classroom before I did and never tried to run again.

But that was not our last confrontation. Rodney did not like homework. We teachers assigned homework as a policy, and we expected that it would be done. Rodney said that if I gave him homework he would burn it. I replied matter-of-factly that I didn't think he would, since he wasn't allowed to have matches, and that even if he did it wouldn't get him anywhere because I had duplicate assignments I would give him. "Well, you son-of-a-bitch, just wait and see," he said. The next morning he was brought to the classroom by a child care worker (attendant). Triumphantly, he threw a tin can on my desk and sneered, "Here's your goddamned homework!" I opened the can. It was full of ashes.

John was almost fourteen. Academically he was at a low, second-grade level. He had been expelled from a special public school class for children with brain damage because he threatened the teacher and other children and had actually beaten another child with a chain. He was on the waiting list to be admitted to the state mental hospital but he was to be enrolled in my public school class for emotionally disturbed children because there was nowhere else for him to go.

When his mother brought him to school the first day, he refused to get out of the car. She coaxed and pleaded, but he refused to budge. She got the principal and he coaxed and pleaded, but John would not talk to him. John's mother and the principal came to me. I went out to the car and coaxed and pleaded, but he would not even look at me. Now what? We decided that we would tell him it was time to come in, and that he was going to come into the building now. He could choose the way he was going to come in — he could walk or we would carry him. Once he had come in and looked over the classroom, he would have another choice — to stay or to go home, and the decision would be his alone. We told him, but he did not appear to listen, and he did not budge. We pulled him out of the car, and he stood up and walked into the building. Five minutes later we were showing him the classroom — he was smiling and talking and decided to stay.

John tested me out in several other ways, and I was beginning to wonder if I was getting anywhere with him. About a month later a new boy entered the class and began the usual testing. Did I mean what I said and would I level appropriate consequences for behavior? At a beautifully timed moment, John went over to the new boy and said, "Look, you might as well do what Mr. _____ tells you to do, because it's for your own good. Besides, he means what he says and if you don't do it you'll only be hurting yourself."

To us, emotional disturbance means getting lost in a tangle of irrelevancies, distortions, unpleasantness, disorganization, and nonproductive activity. Teaching emotionally disturbed children means helping them find their way out of the mess.

Definition

There is no commonly accepted definition of emotional disturbance in children. Many of the terms and concepts in this area (indeed, the term emotionally disturbed itself) have their origins in psychiatry and psychology. Educators have had to make up their own definitions to fit children's behavior in school. Essentially, teachers have defined emotionally disturbed children as those who behave in ways that are considered harmful or inappropriate. The children do things that teachers want them to stop or, on the other hand, fail to do things that teachers think they ought. This would mean, of course, that *all* children are emotionally disturbed, and in a way that is true — all children do most of the things emotionally disturbed children do. The difference is that emotionally disturbed children exhibit behavior that goes to an extreme: they are too aggressive or too withdrawn, too loud or too quiet, too euphoric or too depressed. Furthermore, they exhibit these extreme behaviors over a long period of time, not just for a short while. In addition, disturbed children tend to exhibit behaviors in strange contexts—there is often nothing wrong with what they are doing, only with when and where they are doing it. In short, *emotionally disturbed children behave in ways their teachers consider undesirable or inappropriate, and their behavior differs from that of normal children along several crucial dimensions:* (a) *severity* — the extremes to which their behavior goes; (b) *chronicity* — the period of time over which they exhibit inappropriate behavior; and (c) *context* — when and where they do certain things.

The specific behaviors that emotionally disturbed children exhibit are enough to fill a dictionary. However, Bower (1969) has grouped these behaviors into five classes or types that are relevant to teachers: (a) inability to achieve in school which cannot be explained by sensory or health factors, (b) inability to establish and maintain satisfactory interpersonal relations with peers and adults, (c) demonstration of inappropriate feelings or affect under normal conditions, e.g., laughing when someone is hurt, (d) a pervasive mood of unhappiness or depression, and (e) a tendency to develop physical symptoms, such as pains or fears, associated with their problems.

Classification of emotionally disturbed children has not been very meaningful for special educators. The traditional psychiatric categories have been of almost no value whatsoever in teaching. Factor analytic studies of children's behavior (e.g., Peterson, 1961; Quay, Morse, and Cutler, 1966) have shown that some children are aggressive, rude, attention-seeking, hyperactive, and so forth, and that others are anxious, hypersensitive, fearful, and withdrawn. Others are primarily delinquent, truant, or antisocial according to middle-class standards. The most productive classification system for educators, and the simplest, involves two categories: mild or moderate and severe. Children who are mildly or moderately disturbed can be taught in regular public school classes, where the teacher gets some advice and consultation in behavior management, or in resource rooms, where the child spends only part of the day with a specially trained teacher. Occasionally, these children, who are often labeled neurotic, personality disordered, behavior disordered, and the like, must be taught in segregated special classes, but they are ordinarily returned to a regular class in two years or less. Severely disturbed children, often classified as psychotic, schizophrenic, or autistic, must be educated in special classes in public schools or, more often, in special schools or in institutions. Often, the severely disturbed never enter the educational mainstream.

Prevalence

The U.S. Office of Education estimates that 2 per cent of the school-aged population is emotionally disturbed. Many experts in the field, however, believe that this is an extremely conservative estimate and that a figure of 10 per cent would be much more realistic for mildly or moderately disturbed children (c.f. Bower, 1969). There are no reliable estimates of the prevalance of severely disturbed children, but a figure of 0.1 per cent of school-aged children seems reasonable (Kauffman, 1974).

Etiology

The causes of erratic, disturbing, debilitating human behavior have always been a puzzle which does not appear about to be solved. All that is really clear now is that such behavior stems from the complex interaction of many factors. These factors have been known for a long time, but the exact role that each plays has never been fully understood.

The devil made him do it has always been, especially until the twentieth century, a very popular explanation. The idea that God and the devil battle for control of the mind and body dies slowly, and it is not uncommon, even today, to hear spiritual explanations of and cures for troublesome behavior. There simply is no scientific evidence that divine or demonic powers control the way people behave, but people's belief in such powers is a reality that teachers do sometimes have to contend with.

Something just snapped in his head is another popular explanation of deviant behavior. The belief is that something is biologically wrong with the person — his brain, blood, nerves, and so forth, are said to be damaged or diseased or to be dysfunctioning. Medical science has discovered that such biological factors as malnutrition, disease, fatigue, trauma, and brain damage can cause aberrant behavior. Yet, in the vast majority of cases, even those involving severe disorders, there is no clear evidence of a biological etiology. The search for medical explanations and cures remains, to this day, mostly a matter of speculation.

It runs in the family, the genetic explanation, has never been confirmed. It is known that for some types of severe disturbances (psychoses) the more blood relatives one has who are extremely disturbed, and the closer their blood relationship, the greater one's chance of developing such a disorder. However, this relationship could result from child-rearing practices as well as from genetic factors. The search for genetic contributions to the development of disordered behavior, like the search for other biological causes, is still going on.

He has a sick mind is often the ultimate explanation of those who approach disturbed behavior from a psychoanalytic perspective. A person's mind is thought to get "sick" because of early experiences which cause the person to become anxious and because of his subsequent attempts to defend himself against anxiety. Many experiences and thoughts related to his anxiety are repressed and kept unconscious. There is hardly more scientific evidence for this point of view than for the religious or spiritual explanation, but the notion is deeply entrenched in our culture and because of its pervasive influence it is not easily dismissed.

He just can't seem to find himself suggests that a person does not know or understand his own feelings or perceptions, or has not developed an adequate self-concept. Deviant behavior supposedly arises because the person has not learned introspection, self-awareness, self-regard, sensitivity, and the like. The role of one's feelings and lack of self-awareness *as a cause* of emotional disorders has not been demonstrated in any scientific manner.

He never learned how to get along connotes that disturbed patterns of behavior are learned and that appropriate behavior can be taught. There is a lot of scientific evidence indicating that this is correct, particularly for mild disorders, but it cannot be said that there is conclusive evidence that the explanation is totally correct, especially for more severe disturbances. It is of primary importance to educators, however, because they are in the business of teaching children new patterns of behavior. Inappropriate learning is the only etiological factor that educators are specifically trained to do something about.

In summary, it seems highly probable that most emotional disturbance is the result of many interacting factors, some of which (such as genetics and disease) give children a predisposition to develop disordered behavior and some of which (such as child rearing and schooling) trigger or precipitate behavior problems.

Issues in the Education of Disturbed Children

How to help disturbed children has been nearly as perplexing a problem as how they got that way. Until relatively recently, it was thought that psychotherapists, usually psychiatrists (medical doctors with training in psychiatry) or psychoanalysts (psychiatrists with special training in psychoanalysis) or clinical psychologists (nonphysicians with advanced graduate training in psychology), were best equipped (if not the *only* people equipped) to help disturbed children. Fortunately, most psychotherapists now readily admit that teachers are also equipped to offer extremely significant help to the disturbed child. But the question of exactly *how* teachers can best go about helping — that is the crucial issue now.

There are two contrasting schools of thought about the most effective way to help disturbed children. These beliefs can be characterized by such bipolar adjective pairs as structured/permissive, directive/nondirective, empirical/inferential, behavioral/attitudinal, and the like. For want of better terms we have chosen to call them psychoeducational approach and the behavior-modification approach. Both approaches apply not only to the education of disturbed children but also to other handicapped children and, indeed, to *all* children. In discussing these two ways of teaching — of entering and, hopefully, changing the lives of children — we will first briefly define each approach. Then we will discuss some of the things that the two approaches have in common and some areas in which there are apparently basic and irreconcilable differences between them. Because the psychoeducational-behavior modification controversy is an important and complex one, our discussion may initially appear somewhat "heavy" for this text, but we hope the discussion clarifies the issue and places it in proper perspective.

THE PSYCHOEDUCATIONAL APPROACH

Although the psychoeducational approach is historically linked to Freudian psychodynamic theory, it became evident that one or two hours of therapy per week was both insufficient and too expensive to meet the needs of most emotionally disturbed children; thus clinicians shifted their emphasis to milieu therapy in which the child's total living situation is designed to foster his proper development. Lewin's (1942) cognitive field theory and Redl and Wineman's (1953) residential work with predelinquents contributed significantly to the acceptance of milieu therapy.

Influenced by Caplan's (1961) theory of crisis intervention, Redl (1959) and Morse (1963) formulated the technique of the Life Space Interview for exploiting the meaning of behavioral episodes which occur outside the therapeutic hour. Crisis intervention is based on the assumption that during a time of stress a child is "more apt to search for cues from some aspect of his inner and outer environment to solve his dilemma" (Morse, 1971a, p. 295). During a Life Space Interview the adult and child discuss the crisis, strengthening the child's ego so that he can successfully cope with a wider variety of reality-oriented demands.

When the concept of milieu therapy is applied to schools, it becomes the psychoeducational approach. As an important component of the milieu, the classroom is increasingly recognized as having great potential for bringing about behavioral changes in disturbed children. Berkowitz and Rothman (1960) were early advocates of psychoeducational therapy, but today the more educationally oriented and somewhat less permissive ideas of Morse (1971c) and Fenichel (1966) find wider acceptance among special educators.

Briefly, Morse and Fenichel believe that educational decisions should be based on consideration of unconscious motives and underlying conflicts; that learning should be pleasant and relevant to the child; that group processes and crisis situations should be utilized to develop insights; that the teacher should establish an empathic relationship with the child; and that flexibility is important, although the teacher must enforce necessary limits.

Although Knoblock (1970) and Trippe (1966) plead for "humanism" and Rhodes (1963) supports a social-competence model, each is closely associated with the psychoeducational approach. Their common interests in interpersonal relationships and in a classroom in which a teacher and child work together for goals which the child appreciates serve to make them allies in the cold war against strict behaviorists.

THE BEHAVIOR-MODIFICATION APPROACH

The behavior-modification approach for educating emotionally disturbed children was born of the structured environment formulated for work with brain-injured and hyperactive children (Strauss and Lehtinen, 1947; Cruickshank, Bentzen, Ratzeburg, and Tannhauser, 1961) and of the S-R-S operant-conditioning model (Thorndike, 1903; Watson, 1914; Skinner, 1953; Spence, 1956). Advocates of a behavior-modification approach concern themselves with the relationship between changes in the environment and changes in the subject's responses.

Hewett (1971), Haring and Phillips (1962, 1972) and Whelan (1966) are influential leaders in the campaign to extend the use of behavior-modification techniques in the classroom. Teachers, they argue, must focus on observable behavior as it is manifested in the classroom rather than on internal conflicts and unconscious motivations. The teacher should "(a) select a terminal goal; (b) prepare a series of tasks involving reasonable increments which lead up to such a goal; and (c) through careful selection and presentation of stimuli and consequences, modify the child's behavior and bring it in line with the goal" (Hewett, 1971, p. 360).

COMMON GROUND

Psychoeducational and behavioral educators both believe that it is of primary importance that the child learn the relationship of his behavior to its consequences. Haring and Phillips' (1962) interference theory maintains that individuals live by their expectations of how events will occur. According to their theory, emotionally disturbed children make assertions which have a high probability of being disconfirmed. These children are unable to assess the environmental response to their behavior. "Disordered or pathological or disturbed behavior represents a condition wherein the results of action (feedback) are different from what is anticipated" (Phillips, 1967, p. 153).

Because the child cannot structure and organize his world, behaviorists urge the teacher to structure it for him. A behavioristic teacher provides a consistent environment in which the child can learn to accurately predict the outcomes of his behavior. Rewards follow appropriate behaviors and decelerating consequences follow those that are inappropriate. In a behavior-modification classroom, the rewards provide immediate positive feedback to the child and increase the likelihood of that behavior recurring under similar conditions at a later time.

The psychoeducational approach also concentrates on helping the child develop awareness of the relationship of his behavior to its consequences. However, this approach rejects the inflexible structure of the behaviorist and insists that "at times, daily routines which were established to give security go by the board to capture the emotion of the moment" (Morse, 1971c, p. 331).

Rather than rely on structure and extrinsic reinforcement, the psychoeducational teacher utilizes verbal discussion of behavior to help the child develop insights. One of the major goals of the

Life Space Interview is to lead the child to the discovery that he is responsible for many of the difficulties in which he finds himself. When a child cannot read the meaning of an event in which he becomes involved, the teacher must administer what Redl and Wineman (1953) call the "reality rub-in interview" (p. 497). If the problem has not worked itself out by the resolution phase of the interview, "the adult at this stage begins to inject reality factors in an objective way: implications of behavior, standards, expectations. Reality limits are explained in a non-moralistic way. Why some attention must be given to the behavior is covered, but not vindictively" (Morse, 1971b, p. 488). The adult makes it very clear that to avoid negative consequences the child must change some of his inappropriate behaviors.

While the behavioral teacher uses structure and extrinsic rewards to provide feedback, the psychoeducational teacher utilizes verbal discussion. Both of these techniques help the child change his behavior so that he can increase the gratification he receives from his environment. In both methods the final decision to change rests with the child. In a nonjudgmental manner teachers in both groups provide support and an environment which insures the child the opportunity to recognize that he alone has the power to avoid negative and increase positive consequences. This is what Rhodes (1963) calls making a child "heedful of his own resources and potentialities for the beauty of well being" (p. 61).

Dismayed by the pressure to choose one technique and leave the other behind, students sometimes ask if it is not possible to use both techniques in a single classroom to yield the best possible results? Whelan (1966), a behaviorist, maintains that the "Life Space Interview is a powerful mode of therapeutic intervention if correctly applied but it can also produce negative effects if utilized without cognizance of important behavioral and environmental variables" (p. 39). The increased teacher attention given during the interview may actually reinforce maladaptive behavior. If a child is acting out because he wants the teacher to respond to him, the interview would serve to increase the frequency of acting out. However, the psychoeducators also emphasize that the Life Space Interview should not be used indiscriminately. Morse (1971a) warns that "many events which are crisis to adults are often satisfying, ego-building, and gratifying to pupils" (p. 295).

The interview technique, then, should be reserved for situations in which the teacher can be reasonably sure that the child is not acting out in an effort to receive teacher attention. Teachers can move toward a more effective use of the Life Space Interview by recording and graphing the effects of their attention on the behavior of their students. For students whose inappropriate behavior increases when the teacher attends to it, a delay-interview technique may be preferable; i.e., the teacher should wait until the child behaves appropriately before sitting down to discuss his earlier difficulties. Utilizing verbal-control techniques can help the child in two ways: (a) by increasing his self-control and (b) by fostering his language development. However, if the child is nonverbal or if he does not seem to respond to the discussion technique, the teacher must consider using the behaviorists' alternative, for this child may need structure and extrinsic reinforcement to aid him in his attempt to develop self-control.

Just as the behaviorist can sometimes find the Life Space Interview appropriate, the psychoeducator can search for ways to use structure and external rewards without compromising his values for joint teacher-child goal setting. The last steps of the Life Space Interview, "Strategic Planning" and "New Tool Salesmanship," offer possibilities for harmoniously combining two seemingly opposing techniques. Typically, during the last step of the interview the adult offers the child his assistance and suggests plans for helping the child to avoid a recurrence of the difficulty. A psychoeducator well versed in behavior-modification techniques can make use of both methods at this point. Many children, not yet able to control their behavior without reminders, find a behavior-modification plan, complete with extrinsic reinforcers, very appealing and helpful. Such a plan could also be utilized on a group basis. For instance, the class clown who is not completing his academic work might happily accept a plan in which the other members of the class agree to ignore his clowning behavior until he finishes his arithmetic. The other group members are reinforced for ignoring the clowning. The point is that teachers and children discuss the problem, come to an agreement, and work together to make their classroom a gratifying and productive place. Such a palatable form of behavior modification is not incompatible with ideals of psychoeducators who emphasize the "need to articulate a new humanism for children and teachers that would allow them to function in schools with the feeling that it is their school and their responsibility to create a partnership for living and learning" (Knoblock, 1970, p. 69).

A second area of concern common to the behaviorist and the psychoeducator is that the child not be exposed to stimulation and environmental demands with which he is unable to cope successfully. Cruickshank's (1961) "stripped down" classroom with bare walls and blank study carrels represents the ultimate in classrooms in which stimulation is controlled so that children can attend to academics. The techniques of Cruickshank and the structure of the behaviorist are sometimes shunned by teachers who believe that "manipulation of stimuli and consequences in the classroom dehumanizes the teacher and provides a 'technician' rather than a 'teaching artist' role" (Hewett, 1971, p. 360).

Although the issue of environmental control is very controversial among special educators today, there simply is no either/or choice when it comes to controlling stimuli. Even those in the psychoeducational camp must sometimes resort to extreme environmental controls when dealing with severely disturbed children. Redl and Wineman (1953) emphasize the need for controlling the environment so as to minimize "appeal to impulses the gratification of which would lead to danger or guilt" (p. 83). Redl arranges those tempting elements in children's lives which "bring out the worst in them" into three categories: (a) situational lure, (b) gadgetorial seduction, and (c) contagibility. For instance, to even a normal child, a large open space says "run," a pretty ball says "bounce me," and the sight of other children enjoying acting out says "join us!" To avoid disasters and an "overload on the ego" the teacher of emotionally disturbed children must control environmental stimuli.

Yet teachers should concern themselves with several questions regarding environmental stimuli: How much control, for which child, and for how long? To answer these questions the behaviorists and the psychoeducators both stress starting at the child's level of ability and very gradually moving forward. "A disturbed child's self-image, like that of any other child, is enhanced by experiencing success and diminished by frequent failure. It is imperative therefore, therapeutically and educationally, that we organize a highly individualized program of teaching and a learning procedure and pace for each child to meet his own capacities and needs" (Fenichel, 1966, p. 303). The important consideration here, for both behaviorists and psychoeducators, is that the classroom be carefully arranged to provide each child with success and challenge.

With the structured environment and the shaping technique, behaviorists communicate to the child, "We will not let you fail" (Hewett, 1971, p. 364). In shaping, successive approximations of the desired behavior are reinforced. The teacher asks from a child only what he is capable of producing. He gives the child who is overwhelmed by a whole page of arithmetic only one or two problems to complete. Very gradually, as the child experiences success with arithmetic, more problems are added to each page. The technique of shaping is also useful for developing social skills. The child too shy to talk in a large group is first asked to work with only one other child. After experiencing success with one person, the child begins working with two classmates. By reinforcing successive approximations, the teacher insures that the child will experience both challenge and success. If the child's work is threateningly difficult, the teacher is misusing the shaping procedure.

However loudly they verbalize their disdain for the shaping technique, the psychoeducational group also controls environmental stimuli to provide challenge and success. Redl and Wineman (1953) call their technique "widening the experiential range." They assume that the teacher helps the child gain a feeling of mastery by "offering ego-challenging life situations but ones which are not far away from the scope of ego control" (p. 383).

Psychoeducators and behaviorists control stimulation only when a child cannot function in a more distracting or demanding situation. Neither model advocates leaving a child in such a controlled environment indefinitely. Appropriate use of shaping or "widening the experiential range" means that environmental demands are added gradually to help the child develop responsible behavior which brings him success in the regular classroom and in his natural living situation.

Even within classrooms carefully planned to provide stimulation and demands appropriate to the child's level of development, teachers of emotionally disturbed children confront acting out, defiance, and testing of limits. In these situations behaviorists advocate giving the disruptive child "time out"; i.e., "removing a child from a situation in which he has been receiving accelerating consequences for appropriate behavior whenever he exhibits behavior which is inappropriate" (Whelan, 1966, p. 69). The "time out" may involve placing the child in a small room next to the classroom for a specified time interval or may be limited to simply ignoring the child's behavior (time out from teacher attention).

Psychoeducators condemn behaviorists for using these strong-handed control techniques. Trippe (1966) fears that "assembly line organization and extensive use of surplus repression foster conforming behaviors and deplete children of their creative resources" (p. 25). For the management of disruptive surface behavior, psychoeducators suggest "planned ignoring" when "ignoring makes it easier for it to stop" (Redl and Wineman, 1953, p. 401) and "antiseptic bouncing." A child is "bounced" — asked to leave the room for a few minutes — when his behavior reaches a point where he will not respond to verbal controls. A substitute activity, such as getting a drink or delivering a message, may be provided.

In spite of the similarity of this technique to "time out," psychoeducators insist that their technique is quite different because "there is no intent of punishing the child but simply to protect and help him and/or the group to get over their feelings of anger, disappointment, uncontrollable laughter, hiccups, etc." (Long and Newman, 1971, p. 450).

In looking at the "behaviors received" by each child in a day's time, Redl (1971) emphasizes that "what people really 'do' to each other counts as much as how they feel" (p. 248). This notion applied to "bouncing" indicates that if a child is receiving gratification and is cut off against his will from the source of that gratification, the impact on the child may be the same regardless of whether the teacher calls it "planned ignoring," "antiseptic bouncing," or "time out." Special educators frequently act as if by giving a behavior a new label or by explaining it by a different theory they verbalize away the impact of what is actually done to children. The time has come to focus our energies on an examination of what we do to children rather than on what we call it or how we rationalize it.

Verbal debates at conventions, on campuses, and in journals often serve to polarize educators and to obscure the areas of agreement in psychoeducation and behavior modification. The common features of the approaches must not be overlooked, *for they represent the essentials of classroom management.* Upon this base of "must do's" a teacher examines and selects from the more divergent techniques those which suit his belief system and his children's needs.

DIVERGENT PATHS

Psychoeducators and behaviorists find little agreement on the practice of withdrawing privileges for inappropriate behavior. Redl and Wineman (1953) insist that art, games, recess, and other enjoyable activities are important for developing a child's ego strength and should never be deleted from a child's program. Although behaviorists agree that these activities are essential in the therapeutic process, they believe that pleasurable behaviors should be made contingent on appropriate behavior.

Behaviorists utilize the Premack Principle (Premack, 1959) which, essentially, holds that *any* behavior may be accelerated when it is followed by *any other* behavior that normally occurs at a higher rate in a free-choice situation. In practice, this means that the behaviorist looks for activities which the child enjoys and makes these contingent on appropriate behavior. For instance, the child may be allowed to have ten minutes of free time only after he completes ten arithmetic problems.

Psychoeducators believe that pleasurable activities are the child's "right" and not a "privilege" which can be taken away. They point disapprovingly to instances in which children are kept in from recess for a whole week for not completing difficult math assignments. However, behaviorists also shudder at such nonsense. The use of contingent privileges is, essentially, a shaping technique which insures the child success by rewarding successive approximations of the desired behavior. To apply the technique appropriately, the teacher starts by giving the child a few problems to do to earn a little free time. The amount of work required is geared to the child's level of development so that he does in fact successfully earn his pleasurable activities in almost all cases. The behaviorist gets double mileage out of these things in the school which children enjoy — he makes sure that the child does participate in these important activities most of the time, but he also uses them to reinforce appropriate behaviors.

Motivation is perhaps the most significant issue dividing educational theorists today. Psychoeducators castigate behaviorists not only for utilizing the Premack Principle, but, more importantly, for using trinkets, candy, and other extrinsic reinforcers to motivate students.

Psychoeducators express the importance of joint teacher-child planning and of making learning relevant and pleasurable. The teacher-pupil relationship is considered valuable "not only as an interpersonal feeling, but as a mode of helping the pupil with his motivational defects" (Morse, 1971c, p. 333). The teacher is seen as a facilitator of learning with a primary goal to "develop pupil-teacher rapport and to restore the sense of pleasure in learning" (Morse, 1971c, p. 332). The curriculum is built around the child's interests.

Behaviorists believe that acquiring some types of appropriate behavior is probably not intrinsically fun or pleasurable and that when a child is left to plan his own learning experiences "many learning gaps will exist because learning that needs to be accomplished may never fall within the realm of expressed interest" (Whelan, 1966, p. 65). The use of external reinforcement is a behavioral technique for motivating the student to acquire new behaviors. Once a child acquires new behaviors, however, he may experience feelings of self-satisfaction because difficult tasks have been accomplished. The goal is to gradually move the child from his dependence on extrinsic rewards to the development of intrinsic motivation.

Behaviorists and psychoeducators both hope to help the child become a self-directed and self-motivated learner who, upon becoming an adult, possesses the social and academic skills necessary for independent functioning in a complex, technological society. Psychoeducators fear that reinforcing children extrinsically robs them of their creativity and of the opportunity to become self-directing and self-actualized (Maslow, 1971, p. 169). Behaviorists, on the other hand, fear that giving a child the freedom to choose not to learn appropriate behavior or academics denies that individual the freedom to choose from a wide variety of lifestyles when be becomes an adult. After carefully assessing a student's academic, social, and emotional abilities, the teacher must choose the techniques that will be most successful in teaching the child behaviors that will allow him to become an independent and self-fulfilled adult.

Ponder These

1

Using the criteria of context, severity, and chronicity, describe the conditions under which you would consider the behaviors listed to be "emotionally disturbed" or in need of change. Under what conditions would you consider the behaviors normal?

interrupting conversations

banging head against the wall

screaming

killing another person

scratching oneself

masturbating

eating paper

swearing

saying, "I'm no good. I hate myself."

reading

2

Elmer has a pair of scissors with which he is making deep scratches on the wall of the classroom. You tell him to stop, but he pays no attention. You go to him and take hold of his arm and matter-of-factly say, "No, Elmer, you can't do that." He flies at you, tries to scratch you with the scissors, and screams, "Let me go you bastard!" You lose your grip on Elmer and he runs out of the room. You follow, but lose sight of him as he rounds the corner at the end of the hall. You suspect that he has gone into the boys' restroom. As you enter the restroom you see Elmer perched on top of the stall partition. He has taken off one shoe and is holding it in throwing position. As you approach him he shouts, "Get away from me — you can't make me come down. I'll kill you, you bastard. I'll break my leg, and then my dad will sue you. You come any closer and I'll knock your teeth out." Describe alternative ways you could respond in this situation.

3

Emotionally disturbed children have a way of forcing other people to make decisions for them or about their behavior. Much of the controversy in the field of education of disturbed children concerns the child's right to make his own decisions versus the teacher's responsibility to make decisions for the child. For each of the following problems, specify the decisions you would be willing to make *for* a disturbed child and those you believe should be left to him:

the child is not coming to class on time

the child refuses to read

the child hits others

the child makes loud animal noises in class

the child takes things that are not his

References

Berkowitz, P. and E. Rothman. *The disturbed child: recognition and therapy in the classroom.* New York: New York University Press, 1960.

Bower, E. M. *Early identification of emotionally handicapped children in school.* 2nd ed. Springfield, Ill.: Charles C. Thomas, 1969.

Caplan, G. (Ed.) *Prevention of mental disorders in children.* New York: Basic Books, 1961.

Cruickshank, W., F. Bentzen, F. Ratzeburg, and M. Tannhauser. *A teaching method for brain-injured and hyperactive children.* Syracuse, N. Y.: Syracuse University Press, 1961.

Fenichel, C. Psycho-educational approaches for seriously disturbed children in the classroom. In P. Knoblock (Ed.), *Intervention approaches in educating emotionally disturbed children.* Syracuse, N.Y.: Syracuse University Press, 1966. Pp 5–18.

Haring, N. G. and E. L. Phillips. *Educating emotionally disturbed children.* New York: McGraw-Hill, 1962.

Haring, N. G. and E. L. Phillips. *Analysis and modification of classroom behavior.* Englewood Cliffs, N.J.: Prentice-Hall, 1972.

Hewett, F. M. Introduction of the behavior modification approach to special education: A shaping procedure. In N. J. Long, W. C. Morse, and R. G. Newman (Eds.), *Conflict in the classroom: the education of children with problems.* 2nd ed. Belmont, Calif: Wadsworth, 1971. Pp. 360–65.

Kauffman, J. M. Severely emotionally disturbed. In N. G. Haring (Ed.), *Behavior of exceptional children.* Columbus, Ohio: Charles E. Merrill, 1974.

Knoblock, P. A new humanism for special education: the concept of the open classroom for emotionally disturbed children. In P. A. Gallagher and L. Edwards (Eds.), *Educating the emotionally disturbed: Theory to practice.* Report of a symposium, Topeka, Kansas, 1970. 68–85.

Lewin, K. Field theory and learning. In N. B. Henry (Ed.), *The psychology of learning.* National Society for the Study of Education, 41st Yearbook, Part II. Chicago: University of Chicago Press, 1942. Pp. 215–42.

Long, N. H. and R. G. Newman. Managing surface behavior of children in school. In N. J. Long, W. C. Morse, and R. G. Newman (Eds.), *Conflict in the classroom: The education of children with problems.* 2nd ed. Belmont, Calif.: Wadsworth, 1971. Pp. 442–52.

Maslow, A. H. *The farther reaches of human nature.* New York: Viking Press, 1971.

Morse, W. Working paper: training teachers in life space interviewing. *American Journal of Orthopsychiatry,* 1963, *33,* 727–30.

Morse, W. C. The crisis or helping teacher. In N. J. Long, W. C. Morse, and R. G. Newman (Eds.), *Conflict in the classroom: the education of children with problems.* 2nd ed. Belmont, Calif.: Wadsworth, 1971. Pp. 294–302. (a)

Morse, W. C. Worksheet on life space interviewing for teachers. In N. J. Long, W. C. Morse and R. G. Newman (Eds.), *Conflict in the classroom: the education of children with problems.* 2nd ed. Belmont, Calif.: Wadsworth, 1971. Pp. 485–90. (b)

Morse, W. C. Education of maladjusted and disturbed children. In N. G. Long, W. C. Morse and R. G. Newman (Eds.), *Conflict in the classroom: the education of children with problems.* 2nd ed. Belmont, Calif.: Wadsworth, 1971. Pp. 330–36. (c)

Peterson, D. R. Behavior problems of middle childhood. *Journal of Consulting Psychology,* 1961, *25,* 205–9.

Phillips, E. L. Problems in educating emotionally disturbed children. In N. G. Haring and R. L. Schiefelbusch (Eds.), *Methods in special education.* New York: McGraw-Hill, 1967. Pp. 135–58.

Premack, D. Toward empirical behavior laws: I. positive reinforcement. *Psychological Review,* 1959, *66,* 219–33.

Quay, H. C., W. C. Morse, and R. L. Cutler. Personality patterns of pupils in special classes for the emotionally disturbed. *Exceptional Children,* 1966, *32,* 297–301.

Redl, F. Strategy and techniques of the life space interview. *American Journal of Orthopsychiatry,* 1959, *29,* 1–18.

Redl, F. The concept of a therapeutic milieu. In N. J. Long, W. C. Morse, and R. G. Newman (Eds.), *Conflict in the classroom: the education of children with problems.* 2nd ed. Belmont, Calif.: Wadsworth, 1971. Pp. 244–51.

Redl, F. and D. Wineman. *The aggressive child.* New York: Free Press, 1953.

Rhodes, W. C. Curriculum and disordered behavior. *Exceptional Children,* 1963, *30,* 61–66.

Skinner, B. F. *Science and human behavior.* New York: Free Press, 1953.

Spence, K. W. Theoretical interpretations of learning. In S. S. Stevens (Ed.), *Handbook of experimental psychology.* New York: Wiley, 1956. Pp. 690–729.

Strauss, A. and L. Lehtinen. *Psychopathology and education of the brain injured child.* New York: Grune and Stratton, 1947.

Thorndike, E. L. *Educational psychology.* New York: Lemcke and Buechner, 1903.

Trippe, M. J. Educational dimensions of emotional disturbance — past and forecast. In P. Knoblock (Ed.), *Intervention approaches in educating emotionally disturbed children.* Syracuse, N.Y.: Syracuse University, 1966. Pp. 19–33.

Watson, J. B. *Behavior: An introduction to comparative psychology.* New York: Holt, Rinehart & Winston, 1914.

Whelan, R. J. The relevance of behavior modification procedures for teaching emotionally disturbed children. In P. Knoblock (Ed.), *Intervention approaches in educating emotionally disturbed children.* Syracuse, N.Y.: Syracuse University Press, 1966. Pp. 35–78.

four

Mental Retardation

What does mental retardation mean? At times it can be clever perceptiveness, a happy grin, a belly laugh, an openness, or a blissful naivete. At other times it can be an embarrassed struggle to free oneself from a stigmatizing label, to appear bright, or to dig out of the entanglement of a confusing problem which everyone else seems to overcome with ease. To us, mental retardation means going on a camping trip with Gerald.

After I set up the tent, the rain began to fall. It rained and it rained; it came in buckets, then barrels. We frantically dug trenches around our tent and the holes began to overflow with water. I was disgusted, upset, frustrated, and depressed. I felt that the whole trip had been ruined. Gerald looked like a drowned rat but he was fascinated by the squishiness in his shoes. He laughed as he stepped into puddles, and it was getting to the point where the puddles were becoming pools. I sat disgruntled on a stump, with elbows on my knees and my head in my hands. I began to shiver in the cool breeze. Gerald saw that I was upset. He came over, touched me with a wet, muddy hand and smiled. He sat next to me and tossed a stone in a nearby puddle. Then he looked up at me and said, "Do you think the rain will settle the dust?"

I took a job as a counselor with the Division of Vocational Rehabilitation and was assigned a caseload of clients diagnosed as mentally retarded. During the first week I was escorted by Jim, a fellow counselor, to various job locations where my clients were employed. My most vivid recollection is of my initial meeting with Elmer. The file on Elmer informed me that he was fifty-six years old, that he had been institutionalized until he was past forty, and that he had been castrated. Later, Jim explained that most, if not all, male retarded patients in this particular state were sterilized (castrated) by law. The law is still on the books, but it is no longer enforced; in fact it has not been enforced for over ten years. Jim said that all castrates look the same—pear-shaped, gaining a great deal of weight around the hips just as castrated hogs do. He said that Elmer was an excellent worker, but that on previous jobs he always ate too much and gained weight so fast that they had to terminate his employment and return him to the institution to get his weight down for health reasons. He also informed me that Elmer was basically an honest sort although he was known to stretch the truth a little.

When we arrived at Elmer's place of employment, we found him finishing a day's work and getting on his bike to go home. He *was* a pear-shaped old man, with hips and waist much too large for his height. When Jim introduced us, Elmer was shy, very polite, and quite pleasant to be around. Then Jim began questioning him about his weight. Elmer replied that he did not think he had gained any, whereupon Jim pulled a bathroom scale from the trunk of the state car. We found that within the last two weeks Elmer had gained over thirty pounds. Jim immediately got upset and began talking to Elmer about his eating problem, warning him that if he was not careful he would eat himself to death. He asked Elmer what he had eaten for breakfast. Calmly, Elmer replied that he had only had eggs and toast. After a thorough investigation, we found that Elmer had, in fact, eaten at least six eggs and half a loaf of bread. When asked what he had to drink, Elmer quickly said, "Milk, yes sir, one glass of milk—only one glass of milk. One glass of milk is all I had." Jim retorted, "And how many times did you fill up that one glass?" Elmer looked down at his feet. "Four," he replied. Then he got on his bike and started home. Jim looked at me, shrugged his shoulders and said, "Now you tell me— how do you stop a guy from eating himself to death?"

I worked with Allen every day for six months teaching him how to garnish sandwiches in a high-volume restaurant. He learned very slowly but he was fun and interesting to work with. We always joked with one another. Not even I would ever have guessed that he had a tested IQ of 52.

By about the sixth month Allen was doing his job without any assistance, except for during the rush periods; for the next three months we worked on speed. He became very skillful and could garnish at an impressive rate—except during the very busy times when it was sometimes too hectic, even for me.

Slowly, day by day, pressure began to build. One night when tempers were short at cleanup time Allen started yelling, "Don't touch me! Push, push, push, that's all you do. Don't come close to me. I hate this place! I hate hamburgers! I hate salads! I hate mustard!" With this furious outcry, he flung the mustard container against the kitchen wall and ran out the back door. Impulsively I took off after him. Finally, I caught him by the incinerator on the back lot. He yelled angrily, his voice shaking and hands trembling, "You'd better leave me alone!" Fearing that he might run in front of a car, I stepped closer to reach him. Instantly, he pulled a kitchen knife about ten inches long from his pocket, "Don't come near me, I hate you; take another step and I'll kill you!" Just as suddenly, he dropped the knife to the ground, fell to his knees and wept mournfully. He pulled me close to him, held my legs, and murmured, "I'm sorry. I love you. I'm sorry." Before the night was over, we had talked it out and could complete our cleanup duties together. That was over five years ago. Today, he is still garnishing sandwiches at the same high-volume restaurant, and we are still the closest of friends.

•-0-●▬0-●▬0-●▬0-●▬0-●▬0-●▬0-●▬0-●▬0-●▬0-●▬0-●▬0-●▬0-●▬0-●▬0-●▬0-●▬0-●▬0-●▬0-●▬0-●▬0-

John had worked for two years as a dishwasher and had saved over $2,000 for a motor scooter. I was his employer and had talked with him on many occasions about types, sizes, and colors of motor scooters. One day I took him to several places that sold scooters, and he was surprised to find out that he had enough money to buy any one he wanted. Within the week he bought a red one from a reliable dealer who agreed to teach him how to drive it. When arrangements were made to begin driving lessons, we were suddenly faced with the cold reality that John could not read. He had worked for me for two years, and it was not until that very moment that I learned he was totally illiterate.

I contacted the motor vehicle department and was informed of the types of driver's tests John needed to pass to get a license. The written test could be read to him. I began to teach him lessons from the driver's handbook every day after work. He studied hard, and after six weeks I felt he was ready. He reported for the test and, unfortunately, failed it. I was sure he knew the answers, and through further investigation I found that he understood the material very well but was unfamiliar with the testing procedure of selecting the correct answer from among several choices. I must admit that when the questions and multiple choices were read to me, I also became confused.

So we worked harder. How frustrating for John to own a $2,000 motor scooter and know how to drive it, but be unable to ride it because he couldn't get a driver's license! Three weeks later John took the test again, and this time he only missed two questions. The license was his. He got some insurance and rode to work every day on his proud possession. But I could not help wondering what would happen if he ever had an accident.

About two years after John got his license, I found my answer. He was involved in an accident—a car hit him at an intersection. He was skinned and shaken up but, luckily, not seriously injured. The driver of the car said that John had handled himself extremely well in this unfortunate situation.

He had remembered what to do from the driver's manual and he had followed each step to the letter.

After everything had been taken care of, John called me to come and get the scooter. When I arrived at the intersection, he was sitting alone, bruised and somewhat bloody. His scooter was really a mess. It was scratched, twisted, and crumpled. As we began to carefully slide it in the back of the station wagon, John looked at me with concern and a tear in his eye. "Watch out, don't scratch it," he moaned.

Definition

The most widely accepted definition of mental retardation was developed by the American Association on Mental Deficiency. "Mental Retardation refers to significantly subaverage general intellectual functioning existing concurrently with deficits in adaptive behavior, and manifested during the developmental period" (Grossman, 1973, p. 5). Subaverage intellectual functioning refers to earning a score on an intelligence test two or more standard deviations below the mean. Adaptive behavior refers to such things as sensory-motor, communication, self-help, socialization, academic, and vocational skills. The developmental period consists of the years prior to the nineteenth birthday.

Prior to the inclusion of the consideration of adaptive behavior, emphasis was placed on the intelligence test score for the classification of mentally retarded. If an individual scored in the retarded range on an IQ test, he was classified as mentally retarded even if he functioned in the community, at school, on the job, or with his peers. In other words, once a person scored in the retarded range it was highly probable that he would be considered retarded for the rest of his life.

In the past, many children who were placed in special classes for the mentally retarded because they scored in the retarded range on standard tests and had trouble with academic learning have gotten along well in their community, and with their peers. After leaving school, they have functioned successfully in their jobs, and in some cases married and raised fine families. For these individuals, being labeled mentally retarded served no constructive purpose. According to the AAMD definition, they really were not mentally retarded since they were *functioning in life-type situations within the normal range.*

Not only is it important to accurately define what constitutes mental retardation, but it is equally important to conceptualize it as a *condition* that is *alterable.* For instance, it is possible to be retarded at one time and not to be retarded at another, or retarded in one situation and not in another. Mental retardation is, in many cases, curable. In almost all cases, those who are called mentally retarded are capable of learning far more than we give them credit for. Through training and treatment, some individuals have raised their IQ's significantly above the retarded cut-off point and others have acquired adaptive behavior to such a degree that, were it not for their low test scores, they would be considered normally functioning individuals.

With the current definition, those individuals who experience difficulty with school subjects and score low on tests, yet after school can get along very well on a job in the community, move out of their classification as mental retardates.

The American Association on Mental Deficiency classifies the mentally retarded by levels or degrees of severity, such as mildly retarded, moderately retarded, severely retarded, and profoundly retarded. Table 1 translates the levels into IQ values.

TABLE 1

Levels of Retardation

Levels	Intelligence Test Stanford-Binet	Wechsler
MILD	68–52	69–55
MODERATE	51–36	54–40
SEVERE	35–20	39–25
PROFOUND	19 and below	24 and below

SOURCE: Adapted from H. J. Grossman, (Ed.), *Manual on terminology and classification in mental retardation.* Washington, D.C.: American Association on Mental Deficiency, 1973.

Two terms frequently used by public schools to refer to levels of mental retardation are "educable mentally retarded" and "trainable mentally retarded." The educable mentally retarded are usually those individuals with IQ scores ranging from 55 to 70, and the trainable mentally retarded are usually those scoring below 55. On occasion, public schools will speak of the severely retarded or "custodial," and they are usually referring to persons with IQs below 35.

Prevalence

The United States Office of Education estimates that 2.3 per cent of the population is mentally retarded. These figures are broken down into 2 per cent educable mentally retarded and 0.3 per cent trainable mentally retarded. Most people in the profession of special education agree that today approximately 3 per cent of the population is mentally retarded.

Etiology

It is recognized that retardation can occur from infectious disease, trauma, chromosomal anomalies, abnormalities of gestation, dietary deficiencies, metabolic disorders, blood-type incompatability, poisoning, environmental influence, and many other factors. It has been estimated that over 80 per cent of the mentally retarded fall within the mildly retarded level. Although there is no conclusive evidence as to the causation, it is believed that the majority of those at this level are retarded due primarily to early cultural and social inadequacies. These individuals are referred to as the cultural-familial mentally retarded. The term cultural-familial implies that the causation was a complex interaction of both environmental and hereditary factors.

Realistic Expectations

When mentally retarded individuals are properly cared for and given carefully planned assistance, their potential for achieving, learning, and living is enhanced. In this section we will describe realistic expectations for the mildly retarded and the moderately retarded and the types of treatment and care that are essential for furthering their cognitive, affective, social, and motor development.[1]

---

[1]The expectations have been adapted in part from the adaptive behavior levels cited by Grossman, 1973.

A list of expectations for the severely and profoundly retarded has been omitted because (a) goals for these individuals are a mere extension downward of those for mild and moderate levels, (b) the incidence of such severe mental retardation is low, and (c) most severely retarded people have additional complicating handicaps which must be considered.

Before proceeding, it is important to emphasize that regardless of the severity of his retardation, an individual can be helped and can learn. It is unlikely that the mentally retarded child will blossom or intellectually unfold on his own without special help. Yet retarded behaviors can be ameliorated, and in many cases actually cured with proper treatment. And the earlier we can get involved, the greater our chance of witnessing improvement.

At this point, we would like to mention two investigations which indicate that the retarded *can* learn. In the 1930s it was believed that IQs were unalterable. Skodak and Skeels, in the 1930s, set out to challenge the concept of the fixed IQ and also to demonstrate the effects of environment on the cognitive growth of young mentally retarded children. They selected thirteen children under three years of age for their study. This group was composed of ten girls and three boys with an average IQ of 64. All but two were classified as retarded and were judged by the state law as unsuitable for adoption. Another group of twelve children under three years of age was selected for comparative purposes. The control group was composed of four girls and eight boys with an average IQ of 86. All but two were classified as intellectually normal.

The control group, for the most part, remained in an orphanage and received adequate health and nutritional services. The environment was far from stimulating and was described as meager and desolate. On the other hand, the thirteen experimental subjects were transfered to Glenwood State School and received care on a one-to-one basis from *adolescent retarded patients*. Each adolescent retarded "mother" was given instructions on how to care for her child. The "mothers" were instructed and trained on how to hold, feed, change, talk to, and stimulate the young children. "In addition to the opportunities afforded on the wards, the children attended the school kindergarten. They were sent to school as soon as they could walk. . . . Activities carried on in the kindergarten were more in the nature of a preschool than the more formal type of kindergarten."[2]

---

[2]Braun and Edwards, *History and Theory of Childhood Education* (Belmont, Calif.: Wadsworth Publishing, 1972), p. 216.

Two years later, when the groups were retested, the thirteen retarded children showed a mean gain of 27.5 IQ points, while the twelve adoptees showed a mean loss of 26.2 IQ points. Approximately four and a half years from the origin of the study, eleven of the thirteen experimental children had IQs high enough to be selected for adoption and were thus placed into good homes. In 1965 a follow-up study reported that eleven of the thirteen had married and only one of the eleven marriages had ended in divorce. A total of nine children, all of normal intelligence, were produced from these adults. Of the twelve contrast children, one was deceased, two had married, and one of the two marriages had ended in divorce. Five children were produced from these control-group adults, one of whom was diagnosed as mentally retarded with an IQ of 66. An investigation of educational levels showed that the experimental group had completed a median of twelve grades while the control group had completed a median of less than three. In the experimental group, four of the subjects had one or more years of college work. One had received a B.A. degree and had taken some graduate training. Difference in occupational levels was also great. In the experimental group all subjects were self-supporting or married and functioning as housewives. The control-group occupations ranged from professional and business to domestic service (for the two girls who were never placed in adoptive homes). The control group ended with four of the subjects institutionalized and unemployed. Those who were employed, with one exception, were categorized as "hewers of wood and drawers of water."

Skeels (1966) concluded,

> It seems obvious that under present-day conditions there are still countless infants with sound biological constitutions and potentialities for development well within the normal range who will become mentally retarded and noncontributing members of society unless appropriate intervention occurs. It is suggested by the findings of this study and others published in the past 20 years that sufficient knowledge is available to design programs of intervention to counteract the devastating effects of poverty, socio-cultural, and maternal deprivations. . . . The unanswered questions of this study could form the basis for many life long research projects. If the tragic fate of the 12 contrast group children provokes even a single crucial study that will help prevent such a fate for others, their lives will not have been in vain (pp. 54–55).

The creative and partially successful attempts of Jean-Marc-Gaspard Itard to educate a twelve-year-old savage deserve mention in any chapter on mental retardation. In 1799, a wild boy was captured in the forest of Aveyron, France. The boy, later named Victor, behaved in many ways like a wild animal. Victor did not speak or respond to the sound of gunfire, yet he quickly startled at the sound of a cracking nut. Victor did not seem to feel differences between hot and cold, or smell differences between foul and pleasant odors. His moods swung from deep depression to hyperexcitement. Itard believed that with proper education Victor could be cured. For five years he worked intensively with Victor and then abandoned his goals, concluding that he had failed. Later, the French Academy of Science recognized Itard's significant accomplishments and requested that he publish a report of his work. The result was a classic for the field of education, *The Wild Boy of Aveyron.*

Although Itard had failed to "cure" Victor, many very dramatic changes in the boy were evidenced. Victor's behavior was greatly changed and after much training he was taught to identify various vowel sounds. Ultimately, he learned even to read and write a few words; however, he remained mute.

Itard also concerned himself with the teaching and evaluations of difficult social concepts. He described one of his lessons on justice as follows: [3]

> I thought I ought to test my pupil's moral reactions to submitting him to another species of injustice, which, because it had no connection with the nature of the fault, did not appear to merit punishment and was consequently as odious as it was revolting. I chose for this really painful experience a day when after keeping Victor occupied for over two hours with our instructional procedures I was satisfied both with his obedience and his intelligence, and had only praises and rewards to lavish upon him. He doubtless expected them, to judge from the air of pleasure which spread over his whole face and bodily attitude. But what was his astonishment, instead of receiving the accustomed rewards, instead of the treatment which he had so much right to expect and which he never received without the liveliest demonstration of joy, to see me suddenly assume a severe menacing expression, rub out with all the outward signs

[3]From Itard, JMG, *The Wild Boy of Aveyron* copyright © 1932 The Century Co. and 1962 Meredith Publishing Co., pp. 94-96. Reprinted by permission of Appleton-Century-Crofts, New York.

of displeasure what I had just praised and applauded, scatter his books and cards into all corners of the room and finally seize him by the arm and drag him violently towards a dark closet which had sometimes been used as his prison at the beginning of his stay in Paris. He allowed himself to be taken along quietly until he almost reached the threshold of the door. There suddenly abandoning his usual attitude of obedience he arched himself by his feet and hands against the door posts, and set up a vigorous resistance against me, which delighted me so much the more because it was entirely new to him, and because, always ready to submit to a similar punishment when it was merited, he had never before, by the slightest hesitation, refused for a single moment to submit. I insisted, nevertheless, in order to see how far he would carry his resistance, and using all my force I tried to lift him from the ground in order to drag him into the room. This last attempt excited all his fury. Outraged with indignation and red with anger, he struggled in my arms with a violence which for some moments rendered my efforts fruitless; but finally, feeling himself giving way to the power of might, he fell back upon the last resource of the weak, and flew at my hand, leaving there the deep trace of his teeth. It would have been sweet to me at that moment could I have spoken to my pupil to make him understand how the pain of his bite filled my heart with satisfaction and made amends for all my labor. How could I be other than delighted? It was a very legitimate act of justice and injustice, that eternal basis of the social order, was no longer foreign to the heart of my pupil. In giving him this feeling, or rather in provoking its development, I had succeeded in raising primitive man to the full stature of moral man by means of the most pronounced of his characteristics and the most noble of his attributes (pp. 94–96).

In presenting some of the characteristics and behaviors exhibited by retarded persons, we will discuss some objectives which we believe to be representative of realistic expectations for many of them. Realizing that the retarded differ from one another as much as normals differ among themselves, it is essential to recognize that the discussion will not apply to *all* individuals classified as retarded. The behaviors described are typically displayed at some age level by all children; retarded people just develop at a slower rate or later than do most children.

MILDLY RETARDED

As a terminal goal or expectation for the mildly retarded, we are likely to strive for possible employment in a semi-skilled or unskilled job. The individual should be able to care for his personal needs—selecting proper clothing to wear; bathing and dressing himself; preparing simple meals; performing household tasks such as cleaning, dusting, and laundering; and getting around the neighborhood unassisted. He should be able to carry on everyday conversations, use the telephone, and write a simple letter.

A common problem with the retarded adult is his inability to handle leisure time. Although he may be able to dance or bowl, most of his time is often spent watching television. Thus, developing his interest in active participation in recreation programs is very important. With proper training, mildly retarded adults can learn good health habits (keeping clean, eating balanced meals, getting dental and physical checkups, and the like), money management, and banking.

To attain these adult goals it is best to begin early. We would begin teaching self-feeding to three-year-olds, specifically spoon-feeding skills. At that age we would also be likely to see signs of toilet-training readiness (uneasiness in messy or wet pants). We would work with the child on climbing up and down stairs, running and jumping, and other types of gross motor skills. A language program would encourage the child to name common objects, follow simple directions, and call people by name. (It is important to note that many times a mildly retarded child is not diagnosed as retarded by age three because his development does not differ significantly from that of a normal child.)

By age six it becomes more apparent that the child's development is slow and retardation often begins to be considered as a possibility. At this point we are usually concerned with the teaching of self-feeding with both a spoon and a fork and with working toward less messy feeding behavior. The child's ability to dress himself would also now be of concern, and he would probably still need help with buttons and zippers. Now we would expect him to be partially toilet trained and able to bathe himself with some help. He may now hop or skip, climb steps with alternating feet, ride a tricycle, and throw a ball with some accuracy. We would hope and work toward a speaking vocabulary of over three hundred words. He may engage in simple art projects and dance and participate in group activities and simple games, such as playing store or house.

The mildly retarded child can be effectively educated in a public school system. In the elementary grades he can be placed in regular classes with individualized instruction. A trained resource teacher may be needed to help him with language, self-help skills, and motor development. During the latter elementary grades, and certainly by the junior high level, special provisions must be made for teaching the essential and practical academic subjects. The child may remain with his normal peers in subjects like physical education, music, industrial arts, or home economics, but he may require special programs in language arts, reading, and math. Also, a prevocational program should be begun with instruction in such things as types of jobs available, dress, and reporting to work on time. By high school he may remain with his peers in all subjects in which he can successfully compete, and vocational training should be a major concern. He should be given an opportunity to learn various types of job skills and be allowed to realistically demonstrate his competence by working on various jobs in the community. Job training can be accomplished through a high school work-study program where the student attends school for part of the day and for the remainder of the day is placed on a job for training and evaluation.

Postschool programs are also important. These programs should supply the necessary guidance for helping the mildly retarded person with personal problems that may pop up occasionally, as well as give him time for socialization and recreation. Programs for the mildly retarded must be comprehensive (cover social, motor, cognitive, and academic skills) and continuous (begin early and continue well into adulthood).

MODERATELY RETARDED

The moderately retarded can be viewed developmentally as usually being three or more years behind the mildly retarded. We typically think of the moderately retarded adult as working in a sheltered workshop[1] although a few are capable of holding unskilled jobs. Even into adulthood, these individuals will need a lot of supervision in carrying out routine daily activities. The moderately retarded adult is able to recognize written words and may even be able to read a simple sentence, but for all practical purposes he will be viewed as illiterate. He can carry on simple conversations and can perform such simple household chores as dusting, mopping, and cleaning. He can feed, bathe, and dress himself, but will probably need help in selection of his clothes. Although he can cook simple foods and make himself a sandwich, most of his meals will need to

---

[1]A sheltered workshop is usually a civic sponsored project that hires handicapped workers who are unable to compete in industry. Pressure is reduced by allowing the handicapped worker to work at his own rate. The type of work is usually repetitive and menial.

be prepared for him. By adulthood his gross- and fine-motor coordination will be developed to the point where he will have good body control. His social life will be a constant problem and, if left alone, he will sit idly in a chair or possibly watch television. Although moderately retarded individuals are limited in many respects, they may be interesting, challenging, and, in most cases, enjoyable company.

At age three the moderately retarded are so significantly delayed in their development that most are already diagnosed as retarded. At this age the child usually is not toilet trained; however, he may indicate when his pants are wet and may be ready to cooperate in attempts to teach toileting skills. Self-feeding is messy, but he may become somewhat proficient with a spoon. At three he can stand and walk alone but will need help in climbing steps. He has a vocabulary of from four to six words, recognizes others, plays for short periods of time with others, and communicates many needs with gestures. By age six he begins to exhibit the same characteristics that the mildly retarded person does at age three. For instance, he can feed himself with a spoon (although this may still be messy), and he can drink unassisted. He can climb up and down stairs, but still not with alternating feet. He now can speak two- or three-word sentences and name simple common objects. The moderately retarded individual remains three or more years behind the mildly retarded right on into adult life.

A moderately retarded individual is so intellectually limited and developmentally slow that it may not be to his advantage to place him in a regular school classroom. This retarded person will need a highly specialized program to assist him in developing to his maximum potential. He should usually be educated in a self-contained classroom; that is one room in which all his schoolwork and needs are attended to. This may even include lunch, since feeding must be considered an integral part of his curriculum. At the early ages, the curriculum will include the development of adequate toileting skills. The emphasis of his educational program must be practical, teaching him to take care of himself, get along with others, and like himself as a human being.

As one can see, the mildly retarded person is much closer to the normal child in what he can accomplish than is the moderately retarded. Also, the mildly retarded individual usually looks normal. That is, if you merely see a mildly retarded individual on the street you would not be able to tell he was retarded. This is not the case with moderately retarded individuals who frequently *look* like something is wrong with them; that is, they usually have some observable physical feature that indicates abnormality. The abnormal physical characteristics become more prevalent the more severe and profound the retardation. In addition, the severely and profoundly retarded are usually multiply handicapped.

The characteristics and behaviors which we have reported for the mildly and moderately retarded represent the *upper* limits of the continuum. For instance, it is not unusual to find a mildly retarded individual who is incapable of holding a job and who may even experience a great deal of difficulty remaining employed in a sheltered workshop. The important thing to remember is that *all* retarded individuals *can* learn and *can* grow intellectually, and that the facilitation of this developmental process is greatly enhanced the earlier adequate services can be provided.

It is obvious that being retarded is no prize. Having a retarded child is something parents neither hope nor strive for. The difficulties of parents are often compounded not so much by poor services as by a total absence of services for their retarded children. Initially, parents are often given the "run-around" because no one has the courage to tell them that their child is retarded. Many physicians, who are often the first to notice that a child is retarded, state that parents, once told of their child's developmental lag, are likely to seek other services in the hope that someone will tell them that their child is *not* really retarded after all. The point is that working with the retarded is not easy for anyone — parents or teachers.

In ancient times of kings and castles, the retarded were often used as court jesters, but their condition is nothing to be laughed at. We hope to convey the idea that the retarded are people like the rest of us. Although they often get caught in life's absurdities and amusing circumstances, they have human dignity and deserve our respect. They learn slowly, but they do learn.

Ponder These

1

What are the arguments for and against sterilization of the following classes of individuals:

institutionalized retardates

trainable retardates living in the community

mildly retarded individuals living in the community

2

Think about how you could convince a businessman to hire a retarded adult. For example how would you

request his cooperation (phone or personal contact)

dress for the interview

describe your client; i.e., would you use the term "retarded"?

ask questions about the job description

describe the competencies of your client

3

You are a first-grade teacher in a public school. Your classroom is next to one for trainable mentally retarded children. Your class and the trainable children go to recess together. Ted, a trainable child, frequently soils his pants and your children are beginning to make fun of him, tease him, and laugh at him. What are you going to do about it?

References

Grossman, H. J. (Ed.) *Manual on terminology and classification in mental retardation.* Washington, D.C.: American Association on Mental Deficiency, 1973.

Itard, J. M. G. *The wild boy of Aveyron.* New York: Appleton-Century-Crofts, 1962.

Skeels, H. M. Adult status of children with contrasting early life experiences: a follow-up study. *Monographs of the Society for Research in Child Development,* 1966, *31,* No. 3 (Whole No. 105)

five

Speech and
Language Impairment

Our anecdotes to this point have depicted what it is like to be a teacher of handicapped children. We have not attempted to convey directly what it is like to be handicapped. Almost everyone has at some time or other experienced some embarrassment, guilt, frustration, anxiety, or pride stemming from his verbal interaction with others. Few of us, however, have felt the overwhelming emotions that accompany severe difficulties in oral communication. Listening and talking are such ubiquitous social experiences that we tend to underestimate the handicap that can result from even minor speech deviations. We find it relatively easy to form an empathic relationship with an individual who has an obvious physical, emotional, or mental disorder, but we tend to feel that the individual with a speech handicap suffers no lasting penalty and could easily overcome his difficulty with a little determination. Consequently, we have chosen the following anecdotes in order to call your attention to the feelings and problems of children with speech and language disorders.[1]

---

[1]Charles Van Riper, *Speech Correction: Principles and Methods,* 4th ed. (Englewood Cliffs, N.J.: Prentice-Hall, Inc., 1963), pp. 41-42, 61-63, 72, 181, 384-85. Reprinted by permission of Prentice-Hall Inc.

I must be pretty tough because I'm not in the bug house. The constant experience of starting to say something and never having it come out when I want it to should have driven me crazy long ago. I can't even say my own name. Once in a while I get a little streak of easy speech and then wham, I'm plugged, tripped up, helpless, making silent mouth openings like a goldfish. It's like trying to play the piano with half the keys sticking. I can't even get used to it because sometimes I can fear a word and out it pops; then again when I am expecting smooth speech and everything's going all right, boom I'm stuck. It sure's exasperating (p. 72).

Sometimes when I lie in bed pretty relaxed I almost feel normal. In the quiet and the darkness I don't even feel myself twitching. I pretend I'm just like everybody else. But then in the morning I have to get up and face the monster in the mirror when I shave. I see what other people see and I'm ashamed. I see the grey hairs on my mother's head and know I put them there. I eat but I know it isn't bread I can earn. Oh there are times when I get interested in something and forget what I am but not when I talk. When I talk to someone, he doesn't have a face. He has a mirror for a face and I see the monster again (pp. 62–63).

Even when I was a little girl I remember being ashamed of my speech. And every time I opened my mouth I shamed my mother. I can't tell you how awful I felt. If I talked, I did wrong. It was that simple. I kept thinking I must be awful bad to have to talk like that. I remember praying to God and asking him to forgive me for whatever it was I must have done. I remember trying hard to remember what it was, and not being able to find it (p. 61).

The most wonderful thing about being able to pronounce my sounds now is that people aren't always saying "What? What's that?" I bet I've heard that fifty thousand times. Often they'd shout at me as though I were deaf and that usually made me talk worse. Or they'd answer "Yes" when that just didn't make sense. I still occasionally find myself getting set for these reactions and steeling myself against them and being surprised when other people just listen (p. 72).

The other boys in the school used to call me "stuttercat" and imitate me whenever I came to school. At first I always managed to be tardy and stay after school to avoid them, but my folks got after me and then I began to fight with them. I got to be a pretty good fighter, but the bigger boys licked me and the teacher punished me when I hit the girls. I still hate girls (pp. 41–42).

My mother always hurried to say the word for me whenever company was in the house. I often asked her not to but she couldn't help herself. It used to shame me so, I'd go up in my room and cry and I never went visiting with them. Sometimes I'd eat in the kitchen when we had strangers come for dinner (p. 41).

After I came to high school from the country, everybody laughed at me whenever I tried to recite. After that I pretended to be dumb and always said "I don't know" when the teacher called on me. That's why I quit school (p. 42).

Every time I'd ask for a job a funny look would come over their face and some of them would say no right away even before I finished what I was going to say. Some of the others, and one of them was a stutterer too, just waited til [sic] I finally got it out and then they'd shake their heads. One store-keeper was so sympathetic I could hardly get out of there fast enough (p. 42).

0━0━0━0━0━━0━━0━━0━0━0━0━0━0━0━0━0━━0━━0━━0━0━0━0━0━0━0━0━0━0━━0━━0━0━0━0━0━0━0━0━0━0━0━0━0

Yesterday, when we made that tape recording of my new voice and I heard it, I felt all mixed up inside. I told you it sounded much better, and it does. Compared to my old voice, it's a great improvement. But it isn't ME! It just isn't. I sound like a phony or like an actor playing a part. I know it's better but I don't want to talk so strangely. I just couldn't keep my appointment with you today because I'm so upset about it. I'm even thinking of quitting. I know you said I'd get used to it, but right now I don't think I ever could (p. 181).

0━0━0━━0━━0━0━0━0━0━0━0━0━0━0━0━━0━━0━━0━━0━0━0━0━0━0━0━0━0━0━0━━0━━0━0━0━0━0━0━0━0━0━0

THERAPIST. When you were stuck that time, what were your feelings?

SUBJECT. I don't know. All, All mmmmmmmmmmmmmixed up, I ggggguess.

THERAPIST. You probably felt helpless . . . sort of as though your mouth had frozen shut . . .

SUBJECT. And, and and I cccccouldn't open it. Yeah.

THERAPIST. You couldn't open it. It was almost as though you had lost the ability to move a part of yourself when you wanted to . . . Sure must be frustrating . . .

SUBJECT. Sssure is. BBBBBurns me up. I, I, I, jjjust hate mmmmm . . . Oh skip it . . . I don't know.

THERAPIST. (Acceptingly) It almost makes you hate yourself when you get stuck like that.

SUBJECT. Yeah, dih-dih-sigusted with mmmmmmyself and everything else . . .

THERAPIST. Some stutterers even find themselves hating the person they are talking to.

SUBJECT.   Yyyyeah, I, I, I, I, I wwwwas huh-huh-huh-hating yyyyyyyyyyyyou just then.

THERAPIST.   Uh huh. I know.

SUBJECT.   (Blurting it out) How, how come you know all these th-things? (pp. 384–85).

Speech and language disorders are particularly complex problems. For this reason speech clinicians typically receive rigorous training and are required to meet high professional standards. Correction of speech and language disorders is carried out in many different, often multidisciplinary settings. Therefore, in many universities, training programs for speech clinicians are located in departments other than special education, such as departments of speech pathology and audiology. Basic knowledge of speech and language disorders and of their correction is important for all special educators because many children with other primary handicaps, such as mental retardation and emotional disturbance, also experience difficulties in speech and language.

Definition and Etiology

Unfortunately, the identification of a speech or language impairment is often a matter of subjective judgment. Just how much a language or speech pattern must differ from normal before it becomes a disorder often depends upon characteristics of both the listener and the speaker. For instance, a mother having grown accustomed to her nine-year-old's unusual articulation may overlook the fact that the child's speech is unintelligible to his peers. Moreover, whether a speech difference is considered a disorder depends upon the age of the speaker. That is, in a three-year-old faulty articulation is normal and certainly would not be thought of as a disorder, as it might be for an older child.

In spite of difficulties involved in precisely defining speech and language disorders, usable definitions have been developed by speech pathologists. Communication disorders which have been defined include oral language and speech disabilities.

The causes of speech and language disorders may be biological or functional. Biological etiologies may involve structural malfortions or neurophysical dysfunction; e.g., cleft palate, cleft lip, enlarged adenoids, hearing impairment, cerebral palsy, and so forth. Most disorders of speech and language, however, have no known biological cause and are, therefore, termed functional disorders.

ORAL LANGUAGE DISABILITIES

"Disability in oral language occurs when an individual is unable to comprehend meaningful ideas which have been spoken or when he is unable to use spoken words to effectively express meaningful ideas" (Hull and Hull, 1973, p. 303). Language disabilities associated with neurological problems are sometimes referred to as aphasia. Children with this type of language disability have difficulty understanding and using spoken language because their brains simply do not receive and process information in a normal way. Other children may develop oral language more slowly than is normal because they have lived in environments where they have heard poor language models and have not needed to develop the language skills expected in most schools. Still other children fail to develop oral communication skills due to their mental retardation or severe emotional disturbance. Language delay in these children does not result from specific neurological damage or lack of stimulation; rather, their inability to use oral language is associated with an overall lag in development. Finally, some children may be handicapped in their ability to use oral language due to significant hearing impairments. Those children whose hearing impairment precedes the development of their oral language are more severely affected than children whose hearing loss postdates their acquisition of oral communication.

DEFECTIVE SPEECH

"Speech is defective when it deviates so far from the speech of other people that it calls attention to itself, interferes with communication, or causes its possessor to be maladjusted . . . . Speech is defective when it is *conspicuous, unintelligible,* or *unpleasant*" (Van Riper, 1963, p. 16). It is important to remember that "conspicuous," "unintelligible," and "unpleasant" are subjective descriptors. Just as beauty is in the eye of the beholder, defective speech is in the ear of the listener. Speech can vary along numerous dimensions, several of which are the basis of classification of speech disorders.

Articulation. The way sounds are produced and put together to make words is called articulation. Articulation disorders consist of omissions (e.g., "tha" for "that"), substitutions (e.g., "thnake" for "snake"), and distortions (e.g., "s" produced by lateralized emission of air). Children with articulation difficulties are sometimes described as using baby talk, being "tongue-tied," or not "talking plain." The causes of articulation difficulties include slow development, missing teeth, cleft palate or lip, neurological impairment, emotional problems, and especially faulty learning. In the vast majority of cases with which a speech clinician works, the articulation problem is functional; i.e., the etiology is unknown. It must be remembered that some children may not master *all* of the speech sounds until approximately eight years of age. It is not uncommon or pathological for children between the ages of five and eight to misarticulate some sounds, and for children younger than three years of age to be unintelligible except to their parents. When evaluating a child's articulation, one must always keep in mind the child's overall developmental level.

Voice. Phonation or voice is the tonal or musical quality produced by vibration of the vocal folds. Voice can vary along one or more of at least five dimensions: pitch, loudness, flexibility, and quality. The child's voice may consistently be too high- or low-pitched, too loud or too soft, too much a monotone, or too breathy, harsh, or hoarse. These disorders of voice may be caused by malformation, injury or disease of the vocal folds, psychological factors, hearing loss, and so forth. Damage to the vocal folds can result from the child's persistent misuse of his voice, e.g., excessive screaming. It is also possible for voice disorder to arise from faulty learning.

Stuttering. Normal speech is perceived as relatively fluent or smooth-flowing. Dysfluencies or disruptions in the flow of speech are one aspect of stuttering. Normal speech contains disruptions of rhythm or dysfluencies, but when these occur so frequently and severely that the listener's attention is drawn to them and they interfere with communication, the speaker may be considered to have a speech problem. The speech disruptions which characterize stuttering include repetitions or prolongations of a sound, word, syllable, or speech posture and/or avoidance and struggle behaviors. Stuttering involves social, emotional, and physiological reactions in both speaker and listener and appears to be caused, in most cases, by a complex interaction of factors.

Speech disorders associated with hearing impairment. If a child has a significant hearing impairment his speech may be characterized by voice disorders and many errors of articulation. He is most likely to misarticulate those sounds which are unvoiced and are of a high frequency such as "s," "f," "p," "t," and "sh."

Speech disorders associated with cerebral palsy. The brain damage referred to as cerebral palsy may make it difficult or impossible for the child to control the muscles necessary for proper phonation and articulation. Consequently, his speech may be characterized by fluctuating patterns of pitch, timing, intensity, and articulation.

Speech disorders associated with cleft palate or cleft lip. Cleft palate is a structural defect in the palate or roof of the mouth which may make it difficult or impossible for the individual to close off the nasal air passage as is necessary for proper articulation. Speech associated with an unrepaired or inadequately repaired cleft palate is hypernasal; i.e., too much air escapes through the nose as the person talks. Cleft lip (often inappropriately referred to as "harelip") is a structural defect in the upper lip which, if unrepaired, may also result in defective articulation. Both cleft palate and cleft lip result from failure of the bone and/or soft tissue of the palate or lip to fuse during approximately the first trimester of pregnancy.

Speech disorders associated with mental retardation. Mentally retarded children may exhibit speech behavior characteristic of children of a much younger chronological age, as one would expect given their generalized developmental delay. Mentally retarded children may be more likely, however, to develop greater problems in speech than normal children of the same developmental age.

ADDITIONAL CONSIDERATIONS

We have outlined only major disorders of speech and language and the major etiological factors contributing to these conditions. There are other less common or more specific disorders and etiological factors which are beyond the scope of this chapter. Moreover, within each of the broad categories we have outlined, there is wide variation in degree or severity of handicap. Additionally, a given individual's speech may be disordered by more than one of the conditions which we have discussed. For more detailed treatment of speech and language impairments see Perkins (1971), Travis (1971), or Van Riper (1972).

Prevalence

It is estimated by the United States Office of Education that 3.5 per cent of the school population is speech handicapped. Most speech pathologists, however, believe that 5 per cent is a more realistic figure. The American Speech and Hearing Association (ASHA) has estimated the percentage of children between the ages of five and twenty-one years having specific speech defects as follows:[2]

functional articulation disorders	3.0
voice disorders	0.2
stuttering	0.7
speech associated with cleft palate	0.1
speech associated with cerebral palsy	0.2
retarded speech development	0.3
speech associated with impaired hearing	0.5

The prevalence of language disorders is difficult to estimate and there are no satisfactory figures for this impairment at present.

Speech Correction in the Schools

Speech clinicians perform their services in a wide variety of settings, including elementary and secondary schools, speech and hearing clinics, and hospitals. Schools serve the largest number of children: the United States Office of Education in 1969 estimated that over one million speech-handicapped children were receiving services at the elementary- and secondary-school levels. In the years since 1969, because school administrators have begun to realize the importance of the services of speech clinicians, there has been a sharp rise in the number of school children being served.

School speech and language programs are the most feasible means of providing services to children. Working together, teacher and clinician can identify and provide assistance to large numbers of children who otherwise might never be taken to a speech center.

---

[2]"Speech Disorders and Speech Correction," *Journal of Speech and Hearing Disorders* 17 (1952): 130. For more recent statistical data see F.M. Hull, P.W. Mielke, R.J. Timmons, and J.A. Willeford, "The National Speech and Hearing Survey: Preliminary Results," *ASHA* 13 (1971): 50–9.

Unfortunately, because most school systems continue to hire too few speech clinicians, only those children with the most severe speech handicaps are served by them on a regular basis. Teachers, then, play a vital role in assisting those children not seen regularly by the speech clinician. After a careful assessment of the child's speech, the clinician can recommend activities on which the child can work in the classroom. Only through the cooperative efforts of teacher and clinician can assistance be provided for all children with speech and language handicaps.

STUTTERING: THE GREAT ENIGMA

No problem in speech pathology is as much a puzzle as is stuttering. Although it has received more research attention than has any other problem in speech and language development still very little is known about the cure and even less about the cause of pathologically dysfluent speech. Among the few things we do know are the following:

1. Stuttering is a natural phenomenon of childhood. In learning speech and language all children become dysfluent to some degree. Many children develop patterns of dysfluency which are transitory but do, nevertheless, cause their parents grave concern. In almost all cases, stuttering begins before adolescence, and by college age approximately three-fourths of formerly stuttering children are no longer considered stutterers.

2. Stuttering is more prevalent among boys than girls. Various studies have reported boy: girl ratios ranging from 3 : 1 to 8 : 1.

3. Stuttering runs in families. This may or may not be due to hereditary factors. One should remember that religious beliefs also run in families.

4. There are numerous theories of stuttering, none of which is sufficient to explain all cases. Hereditary, psychodynamic, organic, and learning theories have been proposed. It is also believed by some researchers that children become stutterers primarily because parents show exaggerated concern for the young child's normal dysfluencies.

5. Although a large number of treatment methods have been applied, none has been universally successful. Therapeutic efforts have included systematic desensitization, negative practice, ego building, psychotherapy, operant conditioning, voluntary control, modification of stuttering patterns, chemotherapy, surgery, hypnosis, and rhythmic speech. While no universal "cure" has been found, it appears that some of the most successful treatments known to date are those based on learning principles.

6. Classroom teachers can help the child who is markedly dysfluent by:
    accepting him as he is
    looking *at* him, not away, when he talks
    encouraging him but not forcing him to talk
    not saying things for him
    building his self-confidence by emphasizing his assets
    encouraging him to participate in group activities
    letting him know that they are aware of but accept his
        problem

Postscript

An individual's speech is one of his most personal attributes. Certainly, as the anecdotes at the beginning of this chapter demonstrate, having a speech handicap can be extremely embarrassing and painful. Noticing that people continually respond more to the sound than to the content of his speech can inhibit a person's desire to communicate his thoughts and feelings. While a child with a speech disorder may choose a world of silence rather than face the disturbing reactions on a listener's face, he can, with help, overcome or learn to cope with his difficulty. At times, he can make light of his own unfortunate situation. Having a speech or language handicap, like having any other handicap, does not exclude a child from the world of fun and humor.

When I was fifteen, I participated with a group of five other boys in a stuttering therapy program. All of us in the group had a common problem — Mrs. Shinn, the lady who worked in our favorite ice cream parlor. We'd go into the store to order a strawberry cone and say, "I want a st-st-st-st-st- . . .," and before we could finish the word she'd hand us a strawberry cone. Sometimes she'd even say, "Yeah, I know, strawberry." Well that's pretty irritating, to have someone think he can always predict what you're going to say. It's even worse when someone finishes a sentence for you. Much as we liked the ice cream she dished out, we all started to hate old Mrs. Shinn. So we thought of a way to teach her a lesson. One day we went into the ice cream parlor one after another. Each of us said the same thing, "I want a st-st-st-st-st-. . ." and just as Mrs. Shinn was about to hand us the strawberry cone we finished, ". . . st-st-st-chocolate cone." From that day on, she always let us finish our orders before she started to dip.[3]

When I was a boy, my parents made sacrifices to give me stuttering lessons. I got pretty good at stuttering after a while. I could stutter in iambic pentameter, a feat that turned the most patronizing grown-up pale, and I could speak my name to the rhythm of the first thirty-two bars of "Tiger Rag." That is top stuttering. I suppose today stuttering lessons, like everything else, are much more expensive, but at that time, when Calvin Coolidge was on the march and the 1930's just a threat, lessons were offered at about $5 an hour and were "guaranteed" to stop stuttering instantly, or at least somewhere on the lively side of the statistical expectancy. The people who administered these courses were and probably still are, great practical jokers. Each stuttering school "arranged" that their method proceed under a form of group therapy. Any stutterer knows that no group of stutterers can be persuaded to stop talking to each other, if only in the hope of picking up a new style such as a stammer or a bilateral emission lisp, the way interested new side men do at a solid jam session. The result of such conversation exchange was a gregarious sort of nervous shock which in no time halted the power of speech altogether.

---

[3]We are grateful to C. Lee Woods, Ph.D., for contributing this ancedote.

At last my parents found the Neurological Institute. The experts there shrugged casually. It was a lead pipe cinch. It seems that I stuttered because of my hands. Essentially, they explained, I was an addled chirognostic. I was right-handed when I should have been left-handed, and whoever had insisted that I use my right hand for eating and writing while I had been growing had scrambled my speech centers. And they were right. It was only a crutch, someone told me patiently, but it worked. Today I can talk fast and long and I hardly stutter at all.[4]

---

[4]From R. Condon, "A Show of Hands," *Holiday Magazine* 36, no. 3 (1964): 12. Reprinted by permission of the Curtis Publishing Co., Indianapolis, Indiana.

Ponder These

1

One judges another's speech to a large degree on the basis of what he is accustomed to hearing. Which, if any, of the following individuals would you judge to have defective speech? What specific characteristics of their speech distract you from the content of what they have to say?

George C. Wallace   George Burns
Edward Kennedy   Jimmy Durante
Ronald MacDonald   Truman Capote
Shirley Chisolm   William F. Buckley, Jr.

2

Imagine that a parent comes to you with one of the following descriptions of his child's speech or language. What specific questions would you ask the parent in order to help you determine whether the child *may* in fact be in need of the services of a speech clinician?

"Now my little boy — he just don't talk plain so you can understand him."

"Melinda stutters."

"Fred sounds like he's talking through his nose."

"I don't know what's the matter. She just hardly ever talks. I mean almost *never!* She doesn't say more than a couple of words in a day, and sometimes you can't even understand those."

3

To get some idea of what it is like to have a speech impairment, try one of the following activities. In public or in the company of strangers or on the telephone, speak with a severe articulation or voice deviation or with marked dysfluency (stutter). Describe your listeners' reactions and the feelings they engendered in you.

References

Hull, F. M. and M. E. Hull. Children with oral communication disabilities. In L. M. Dunn (Ed.), *Exceptional children in the schools.* 2nd ed. New York: Holt, Rinehart & Winston, 1973.

Hull, F. M., P. W. Mielke, R. J. Timmons, and J. A. Willeford. The national speech and hearing survey: Preliminary results. *ASHA,* 1971, *13,* 501–9.

Perkins, W. H. *Speech pathology: An applied behavioral science.* St. Louis, Mo.: C. V. Mosby, 1971.

Travis, L. E. (Ed.) *Handbook of speech pathology.* 2nd ed. New York: Appleton-Century-Crofts, 1971.

Van Riper, C. *Speech correction: Principles and methods.* 4th ed. Englewood Cliffs, N.J.: Prentice-Hall, 1963.

Van Riper, C. *Speech correction: Principles and methods.* 5th ed. Englewood Cliffs, N.J.: Prentice-Hall, 1972.

six

Visual Impairment

Blindness. What sort of image does this word evoke — dark glasses, a dog, a tin cup, the groping tap of a red-tipped white cane? The word "blindness" is commonly associated with thoughts of helplessness, pity, and a life of eternal blackness. But is this really blindness? What does blindness mean? To us it means, in part, working with people who are blind and forgetting that they can't see.

A young blind couple with whom my wife and I were friends and professional associates invited us to their home for an evening near the Christmas holidays. After a time of visiting, we went to the dining area where we enjoyed some refreshments. The colored holiday lights in the windows created a perfect effect for the late evening treats. The next morning my wife received a very apologetic phone call from an embarrassed hostess. It was not until our host and hostess were retiring for the night that they discovered their light switch was in the off position. It was then that they realized they had fed us in a very dark room.

I had not been at the school very long before Tom made his way to my office, introduced himself, and explained why he wore the dark sunglasses. He wore them for cosmetic reasons — they did not really serve any other function. He chose to wear them so that people would not be bothered by the appearance of his eyes. Tom was just that way — personable, friendly, and concerned about how other people saw him. He wasn't the most brilliant of students in the school; in fact, he had a harder time than most. But you could count on this high school sophomore for getting along with everyone. Several of us on the staff were convinced, however, that Tom would not be fully prepared to exercise complete responsibility for his own welfare upon graduation unless some rather specific learning took place during those remaining couple of years of high school. It appeared that he was quite content to let others attend to his basic needs, and it seemed there had always been someone there if a need became acute. With the assistance of a counselor, a plan was enacted for improving Tom's sense of responsibility and his skills in independent living. Arrangements were made for him to have a part-time job. He went to work, kept his schedule, was paid regularly, and with the help of the counselor set up a savings account at a local bank. It was understood that the money would eventually be used for purchasing badly needed shoes and clothes. After several months of seeming success, I was greeted one day by a very upset counselor who was convinced that her efforts at teaching responsibility had been in vain. After months of hard work, Tom had succumbed to the desire to be like "the other" teenagers. He had withdrawn all of his savings except two dollars and spent the money for one small stereo and several record albums. And he had no idea whether or not he had paid a reasonable price.

What I remember most from my philosophy class in my junior year of college is Joe, a blind student who sat behind me. He was a likeable guy — good sense of humor and very bright. I think he was unable to see at all. He walked with a cane and took all his class notes in braille — I can still hear the peck, peck, peck of his stylus. One class session about midway through the semester, the professor was flamboyantly explaining a complex theory. He scribbled on the chalkboard to assist him in his instruction. As the professor paused for a moment, Joe raised his hand.

"Yes, Joe."

"I don't quite understand."

"What don't you understand Joe?"

"The whole thing. It doesn't make any sense."

At this, the professor spun on his heel and frantically drew diagram after diagram, at the same time explaining the theory eloquently. After about fifteen minutes, the professor turned around and gasped, "*Now* do you see?"

Joe stopped pecking with his stylus and calmly replied, "No, I still can't see, but I understand."

The professor cried, "*Good!*" wheeled around and started drawing again.

Alex was a very unobtrusive individual. You would not expect an outstanding performance from him, but you often got one. He maintained a good academic record, participated on the track team, and dated Vicki until she graduated and left school. Whenever Alex tackled a job he did his best. In addition to the regular academic subjects, he spent several hours each week with an orientation and mobility instructor learning independent travel skills using the travel cane. During the year, it became obvious that Alex was spending time in independent travel beyond that spent with his instructor. His parents reported that they occasionally transported him to a nearby city where he typically spent a good portion of the day walking through various sections of town in an effort to gain experience. The extent of his travels were unknown, however, until an awards assembly held at the end of the year. Alex, armed only with his initiative, the use of his remaining senses, his acquired mobility skills, his own two feet, and his cane had logged *several hundred miles* of travel amid pedestrians, traffic, and all.

Jim, a young junior high student, came to our school after having been blinded in each eye by separate accidents. It soon became very clear to us that he had an affinity for trouble. Altercations with other fellows in the dormitory were frequent and always had to be followed by disciplinary measures. One day, Jim became embroiled in the fight in which his opponent landed a good blow squarely on his head. A day or so after the fight, his teacher noticed that Jim was seeing things she didn't recall his having been able to see a few days before. A trip to the physician revealed that in fact Jim's visual acuity actually had improved! The blow to his head had apparently temporarily caused the lens of his eye to drop into place. Upon observing this most unusual consequence of fighting, the physician pondered it and then commented in his easy, dry manner, "Well, perhaps . . . a new cure for blindness."

Sue, a young college girl, desired a means of independent travel which would permit her greater range than was possible by foot. Being blind, she obviously could not obtain a driver's license. However, she did have enough remaining vision to ride a bicycle. She purchased a bike and began making frequent trips about the college town and into the surrounding country, often riding several miles. On one occasion she made a visit to our home and decided to return to her dormitory by a new route which took her through the downtown area. As she rode the streets through the main business district, she began noticing numerous friendly people waving and smiling from the sidewalks. They seemed to be waving at her. As she continued, the number of people increased. Then there were crowds, looking, waving, and clapping — for her? Finally, she realized the reason for all the attention. She was riding in the middle of a major holiday parade!

Two adolescent friends attending the school went for a brief walk on the familiar sidewalks of the immediate neighborhood

and left their travel canes behind. During their walk they en-
countered an unfamiliar patch of what felt to them like mud.
They giggled and walked through it to "dry ground." Imagine
the frustration on the face of the homeowner as he looked up
from his troweling in time to see two young girls slogging
through his freshly poured concrete driveway!

Sarah wanted to take high school physics but it was not
offered on campus. The local high school offered it but the
teacher there questioned the practicality of such a course for
a student who had no usable vision. With the assistance of
volunteers, the physics textbook was transcribed into braille.
The semester ended, and Sarah was lauded for her excellence.
She received a grade of "A" and was one of the top students
in her class.

Little Teressa, a first-grader, was examining the various objects in a touch-and-tell box. She extracted a number of shapes
from the box and described or named them: "square," "tri-
angle," "circle." Finally, she came to a cube which was different
in shape and texture from those objects she had already
handled. She paused, felt it intensely on all sides, and said, "A
block; What's this? An H and R Block?"

Blind people are, in the first place, people, and they have the
same human experiences and problems of those with normal vision.
Fred dropped out of school at age sixteen, wandered from one temporary job to another, and to this day continues to live in semi-
dependence, returning occasionally from transient friends to find
food and shelter with parents or grandparents. Melissa, attractive,
popular, successful, graduated from high school. After two years
with her guide dog, she completed business college and landed a job
as a secretary.

Definition

Visual impairment is a malfunction of the eye or optic nerve which prevents a person from seeing normally. An individual has a visual impairment whenever anomalous development, disease, or an individual do not function so that he can see normally in at least one of them, the person is considered visually impaired.

The term "blindness" indicates severe visual impairment and usually implies sightlessness; yet every definition of blindness includes varying degrees of vision. In fact, there are more children classified as blind who can see at least a little than there are those who cannot see at all (Jones, 1961). Actually blindness refers to a condition of severe limitation in visual functioning. People who are blind may find that things look dim, blurred, or out of focus. They may have the sensation of seeing only a part of an object or seeing everything masked in a cloud. They may see occasional dark blotches that float or appear to remain in front of the object they are viewing. It may be that they can see things clearly but only straight ahead, as if looking through a drinking straw. Just as there are varying degrees of vision, the ability to use what vision there is also varies among people.

Unlike most other conditions of impairment, blindness has a legal definition. An individual is legally blind when central visual acuity is less than 20/200 in the better eye after correction or when vision at the widest angle subtends an angle of less than 20 degrees. This legal definition is used as the criterion for providing benefits to blind persons through federal programs; e.g., additional tax exemption, free mailing privileges, special materials from the Library of Congress, the privilege of operating vending stands in federal buildings, the opportunity of receiving special educational materials, and benefits from rehabilitation programs.

Although a legal definition for blindness provides an objective criterion for determining an individual's qualification for special services, it gives very little assistance in decisions regarding educational placement or selection of procedures and materials. A functional definition is much more helpful in choosing an educational program. For example, an individual whose vision does not permit the use of print for reading would be educationally blind. However, unless there is need for a definition in order to provide services, it may be advantageous to describe the condition simply as severe

visual impairment and devote more effort to describing the educational procedures and materials required to meet the needs of
the visually impaired child.

Prevalence

The U.S. Office of Education estimates that approximately
0.1 per cent of school-age children between the ages of five and
nineteen are educationally blind and partially seeing. Using this
estimate, there are about fifty thousand children in the United
States who are visually impaired and could benefit from some type
of special education services. One estimate suggested that there are
about 0.02 per cent educationally blind and 0.08 per cent partially
seeing (Harley, 1973).

Etiology

Most of the visual impairments in school-aged children are a
result of events which occurred prior to, during, or shortly after
birth (Hatfield, 1963). A significant portion of the severely visually
impaired children have cataracts (clouded lenses) or retrolental
fibroplasia (caused by excessive oxygen given to infants). Many
severely visually impaired children have eye problems which were
caused by a condition that also affected another biophysical system.
Consequently, for a significant portion of these children, the visual
impairment is just one of several impairments caused by a single
prenatal disorder or pathogenic agent (e.g., rubella).

Visual Impairment in Perspective

The anecdotes at the beginning of this chapter illustrate several
points about visual impairment.

Most visually impaired (most blind) individuals can see. Only
a small portion of those who are legally or educationally blind are
totally blind or without vision. Both Sue and Jim, for example, had
been taught to read and write braille at some point in their education. However, Sue used print material for most of her schoolwork
and recreational reading. Their visual impairment required a greater
expenditure of energy than is normal in reading or examining things

in detail, and they probably could not recognize friends at a distance; however, for most of their activities, they used vision to some degree. They could see and they behaved accordingly.

Most visually impaired individuals have all their other senses; i.e., they are normal. Being visually impaired, even totally blind, does not impair or improve one's sense of hearing, smell, taste, or touch. A severely visually impaired individual is not endowed with a "sixth" sense. If such a person does do some things in different ways from most, it may be a very natural way of using the other senses in the place of lost vision.

Children who are visually impaired can learn to better use all their senses to help compensate for a loss in vision. Sarah is one who learned material for which vision was thought to be necessary by using her other senses well. Many, perhaps most, can read print material visually if provided good glasses and careful, extensive practice.

Most totally blind persons, by making use of hearing, touch, smell, and a specially made cane, can travel alone by foot. Alex and his several hundred miles is a case in point. With good orientation and mobility skills and experience, the person with little or no vision can use his cane as an aid for crossing intersections, taking walks, making shopping trips, and getting to just about any place within walking distance. A blind person's hands help him to learn about a lot of things if he is just permitted to touch, handle, and move objects that are about him.

Often the biggest block to the blind person's living and learning naturally is other people who have normal vision. Family and friends, in their attempts to be helpful, too often forget the needs of a blind person: rather than permit him to take an elbow, they may push him across the intersection; they may take the blind person's order from his sighted friend across the table; or they may insist upon "look, but don't touch."

As a group, people who are visually impaired comprise a normal range of personalities, interests, and abilities. Some visually impaired people are gifted, some are retarded, and many are normal. There are those who are emotionally disturbed and others with learning disabilities. There are visually impaired athletes as well as scholars. There are those who are socially adept, delinquent, prolific, dull, fascinating, obnoxious, or anything else.

Severely visually impaired people have been successful in nearly every activity and vocation. However, society still judges these people not so much by their abilities as by their perceived differences. Because they are judged incapable *before* the fact, severely visually impaired adults often find locating any job difficult and obtaining desirable employment nearly impossible.

Severe visual impairment can handicap a person in his early experiences and in his ability to get from place to place. Important early experiences can be denied the visually impaired child if he is not permitted to be active and to use all of his senses to the maximum. Tom's lack of early experiences may have contributed to his difficulties in school. In fact, Tom never learned to tie his shoes until he was in high school. He was likely a slow learner, but his inability to perform certain tasks was noticeably out of step with his general level of development. An active childhood and a preschool program are important factors in assuring normal development for the visually impaired child.

The difficulty in moving from place to place is one of the most direct handicaps caused by visual impairment (Bateman, 1967). Sue was only limited in her ability to operate a motor vehicle, but Alex and Melissa's visual impairment caused a direct mobility handicap. They both learned skills however, which permitted them to do what would otherwise have been impossible. Each adapted in a different way but with equal success; Alex worked alone with his cane and Melissa worked with the assistance of a guide dog.

Visual impairment can occur as one of the impairments in a multiply handicapped person. In about half of the cases of severe visual impairment, the visual impairment is probably the only handicap. In the remaining cases, visual impairment occurs as one of several difficulties in multiply handicapped persons.

The child with multiple impairments presents a unique educational problem. In many cases, particularly if the impairments are severe or profound, instruction must be highly individualized. Impairments come in all degrees of severity and in nearly every possible combination. Each additional impairment presents its own unique hurdle to normal growth and development in addition to the problems which result from the particular combination of impairments.

Little is understood about the multiply impaired child, and for some too little has been done to assure maximum potential for development.

Education of visually impaired children has engendered a quiet debate: residential versus day-school education. Until the midpoint of this century, the majority of severely visually impaired children who received a quality education were educated at residential schools for the blind. Since that time, increased numbers of severely visually impaired children are being educated in local day-school programs (Jones and Collins, 1966) and attendance at residential schools has been dwindling. An increasing percentage of those enrolled in residential schools are children with multiple impairments (Wolf, 1967). While it is doubtful that most residential schools will begin going out of business, their future role is in question.

Whether the residential schools remain schools for the blind or become schools for the multiply impaired, the issues in the residential versus day-school controversy still apply. The following are some of the major considerations of the debate:

1. Favoring day schools
   a. It is important that children live at home with their families.
   b. Dormitory living is detrimental to healthy development.
   c. Segregation from normally seeing peers deprives visually impaired children of important experiences needed for normal development.
   d. Larger local high schools can provide a wider range of curricular offerings than most small residential schools.

2. Favoring residential schools
   a. Only the residential school is in a position to directly influence what learning takes place between the end of one school day and the beginning of the next.
   b. The child can receive more individualized instruction than is possible in the day schools where classes are often much larger.
   c. Education will be better where the teachers can devote their entire interest and training to working with those who are visually impaired.
   d. Where the number of children or the number of handicapping conditions increases, the visually impaired will become a neglected minority, eventually losing out on educational services and materials as money is spent elsewhere.

To summarize, in whichever setting visually impaired children are educated, it is of primary importance that their needs as *children* not be overlooked.

Ponder These

1

If a child with no travel vision entered your class, what specific things would you have to teach him in order for him to adapt successfully to the classroom? How might you and the children in your class have to change your habits or behaviors to facilitate the child's adaptation?

2

Imagine that you are a self-sufficient blind adult. How would you feel about receiving a special tax exemption simply because you are categorized as "legally blind"? Would you work for legislation providing special exemptions for persons categorized in other ways as handicapped (e.g., deaf)?

3

If you suddenly lost your vision, what special problems would you encounter in performing such everyday activities as eating, dressing and grooming, toileting, communicating, and getting around? What would you do for recreation?

References

Bateman, B. D. Visually handicapped children. In N. G. Haring and R. L. Schiefelbusch (Eds.), *Methods in special education*. New York: McGraw-Hill, 1967.

Harley, R. K. Jr. Children with visual disabilities. In L. M. Dunn (Ed.), *Exceptional children in the schools: Special education in transition*. New York: Holt, Rinehart & Winston, 1973.

Hatfield, E. M. Causes of blindness in school children. *The Sight-Saving Review*, 1963, *33*, 218–33.

Jones, J. W. *Blind children, degree of vision, mode of reading*. Washington, D.C.: United States Government Printing Office, 1961.

Jones, J. W. and A. P. Collins. *Educational programs for visually handicapped children*. Washington, D.C.: United States Government Printing Office, 1966.

U.S. Office of Education. *Estimated number of handicapped children in the United States, 1971–72*. Washington, D.C.: U.S. Office of Education, 1971.

Wolf, J. M. *The blind child with concomitant disabilities*. New York: American Foundation for the Blind, 1967.

seven

Hearing Impairment[1]

At the age of three David began undergoing speech therapy. Each week his mother took him to the session, sat through as an observer, and then took him home. At the first visit the therapist, who was aware of the fact that David had a little experience in speechreading, chose to test the skills by initiating a simple command, "close door." David watched the therapist's face intently but made no move to carry out the command. The command was repeated and, again, no response. This continued for a while until it became obvious that both the therapist and David were confused. Not daring to initiate other commands or try other words under the circumstances, the therapist suggested to the mother that perhaps David was disturbed by the new situation. Calmly looking into the therapist's eyes the mother patiently suggested, "try *'shut door.'* "

>••<

We were being trained to be teachers of the deaf. We had completed our course work and were preparing to do student teaching at a residential school. We had been trained strictly in teaching speech and speechreading (lip reading) without the use of signs or gestures. However, students and staff at the

[1]Special gratitude is extended to Lois Schoeny and Lynne Mann, experienced teachers of hearing impaired children, who kindly provided anecdotal material used in this chapter.

school made considerable use of manual signs and finger spelling, none of which we understood. A few of us were given assignments at the secondary level which was particularly difficult since the use of signs at that level was considerable.

We were all having difficulty mastering sign language in addition to our student-teaching assignments. To improve our ability we practiced these skills by reading the Ann Landers column to our fellow student teachers in the evening. It was a laborious task and each day's column seemed to take forever.

During our learning period, one of my fellow student teachers returned to our domitory at the end of an exhaustive day. She was embarrassed, concerned, and wondering aloud, "What do they think of me?" Only after considerable coaxing did the story come out. Her responsibility was to teach arithmetic. Because of her difficulty with manual signs and the inability of many students to speechread, she had devised a plan to use the overhead projector in writing out each problem for the students to work. Things went well until she indicated the operation of addition by writing the plus sign (+). This was greeted by a room full of blank faces. Try as she might, she was unable to make the children understand that they were to add. Exasperated, she finally decided to resort to finger spelling the word "add." Suddenly the room was astir with children's snickering and laughing. What had she done? There in the middle of a lesson, standing before all those young attentive faces, she suddenly realized that she had just signed the letters "a-s-s"!

I had just completed a university program in teaching the deaf, and the summer was mine to relax and prepare specifically for my first teaching experience in the fall. I was well armed with techniques and materials and very anxious to apply them to my class of early elementary children.

The first day of school finally arrived. Was I prepared! The room was ready and I was at school well before the hour. My course work and student-teaching experiences had taught me well that deaf children at the age of those I was soon to teach have difficulty in reading and require much work if they are even to be able to speak. I also knew that a part of teaching deaf children involves surrounding them in a world of language.

I thought that while my children might be unable to hear me and produce only the most gross approximations to words in their speaking, I would greet each child at the door with a "good morning." As they entered the room I positioned myself so that my face was clearly visible and I carefully spoke and formed the words "good morning." I anxiously watched each small face for any sign of recognition or attempt at response. Response I got. To each greeting there was a well-spoken "Good morning, Mr. _____." I had just introduced myself to my "deaf" class, only to discover that they were not deaf but were an excited, talking, hearing group of "hearing impaired" children.

I was most impressed with Phyllis' emotional maturity and language facility. Her *speechreading* was excellent and proved a boon to those of us who were her close friends. She often related conversations which were taking place well out of ear-shot, across the dining room or lounge. Besides working at her studies, Phyllis was enjoying an active social life. During the course of college she began dating one special fellow. After a period of time during which she had been seeing her friend quite regularly, she returned one night appearing a little dis-couraged. She and John had broken up. As she explained, going places together was enjoyable, and they liked each other's company, but always having to say "good night" or exchange "sweet nothings" while sitting under a *light* was just too much for John to handle.

Definition

Whenever a child is prevented from hearing environmental sounds because of malfunction of the ear or of the associated nerves, he experiences some form of hearing impairment. Hearing impairments can be temporary or permanent, severe or mild. In discussing the problem of defining and classifying hearing impairment, Myklebust (1964) proposed that four variables be considered: (a) degree of impairment, (b) age at onset, (c) cause, and (d) physical origin. The variables of degree of impairment and age at onset have the most direct relevance for education. Both are accounted for in the definition provided by Streng, Fitch, Hedgecock, Phillips, and Carrell (1958).

> The child who is born with little or no hearing, or who has suffered the loss early in infancy before speech and language patterns are acquired is said to be deaf. One who is born with normal hearing and reaches the age where he can produce and comprehend speech but subsequently loses his hearing is described as deafened. The hard of hearing are those with reduced hearing acuity either since birth or acquired at any time during life (p. 9).

As is apparent from this definition, development of spoken language is related to hearing impairment and is of major concern to the educator.

Prevalence

It is estimated that 5 per cent of the school-aged population possess some degree of hearing impairment (Silverman and Lane, 1970). Of this 5 per cent, approximately 1 to 1.5 per cent are in need of special education services (McConnell, 1973). As the figures reveal, there are a great number of children who have hearing impairments that need attention but who do not require special education service because their impairment is minor or correctable.

Etiology

In a study of school-aged, hearing impaired children enrolled in special education programs, more than half had impaired hearing at birth with nearly 28 per cent of all cases being hereditary in origin (Myklebust, 1964). In the same study, etiology was undetermined for approximately 38 per cent.

Impairments of hearing in the outer or middle ear (conductive), even when that portion of the auditory system is totally nonfunctional, leave some potential for using residual hearing (Myklebust,

1964), whereas impaired hearing resulting from loss of inner-ear or nerve functions (sensory-neural) can be a more serious, irreversible type of hearing loss.

Hearing impairments can result from a variety of causes. Excess ear wax and placement of small objects in the ear by children are frequent causes of conductive hearing impairments, as is otitis media, inflamation of the middle ear (Davis, 1970). Some childhood diseases which involve viral infections of the upper respiratory tract can also cause hearing loss. Other causes include the use of certain antibiotics (McGee, 1968), excessive exposure to loud noises, viral infections of the pregnant mother prior to the child's birth, and Rh incompatibility (Davis, 1970).

Impressions

Many times people have certain wrong impressions about hearing impaired children, such as (a) "deaf" children cannot hear, (b) children who cannot hear cannot talk, and (c) "deaf" children are retarded. These three notions have direct educational and social implications; therefore, they will receive focal attention in this chapter.

Deaf children cannot hear. Children classified as profoundly or totally deaf may still have some ability to hear. They may be able to hear loud noises such as automobile horns or slamming doors. The ability to hear even this much may provide the child with vital information to alert or warn him of danger. Of all hearing impaired children, relatively few can properly be labeled profoundly deaf. Many have enough usable hearing to develop language.

There are two ways in which a hearing impaired child can be helped with respect to the information that he receives. First, he can be helped to understand and use what sounds he can hear. Then, of course, if the hearing impairment is such that the variety of sounds can be increased through amplification, the child can be given access to more information through use of the hearing aid. For these reasons, it is important that the hearing impaired child be identified as soon as possible, and that he be exposed to experiences in listening and interpreting sounds (auditory training).

Deaf children cannot talk. In language acquisition, receptive precedes expressive language. The profoundly deaf child, because he cannot receive language aurally, will be handicapped in his expression of the language. However, children with all degrees of hearing impairment are able and usually do learn to communicate.

With amplification and auditory training, hard-of-hearing children can usually use their hearing to develop spoken language. They can and do talk. Some deaf children, with the benefit of little or no residual hearing, are able to develop successful speechreading (lip reading) and some speaking skills. While ability in speechreading skills may vary, the acquisition of clear, intelligible speech by the child born profoundly deaf is usually a laborious task. Both receptive and expressive language is available to the profoundly deaf through the use of manual sign language and finger spelling.

For a long time there has been great controversy over whether educators should rely strictly upon oral language (oralism) or should use manual sign language (manualism) when teaching deaf children. Unfortunately, the issue has not, as yet, been resolved. There is some trend toward a combined use of oral and manual methods in a procedure identified as "total communication."

Deaf children are retarded. The measurement of intelligence has traditionally relied heavily upon language, and language is precisely the area of greatest handicap for the seriously hearing impaired child. Both professionals and laymen have wrongly inferred that because hearing impaired persons evidence a language deficit there may also be an intellectual or cognitive deficit. More recent, broader conceptualizations of intelligence include considerations of non-verbal or performance aspects (Myklebust, 1964). With language factors accounted for, the intelligence of hearing impaired children approximates the norm for hearing children (McConnell, 1973; Wiley, 1971).

Observations of behavior of the profoundly deaf may also give the impression of retardation. When a child does not respond to another's voice, responds unusually to loud noises, demonstrates problems in balance, or produces strange vocalizations, he may mistakenly be judged mentally retarded. These behaviors alone or in combination actually may indicate serious hearing problems. The alert observer should have the child checked for hearing loss.

Cognition and Communication

The mistaken impressions of the preceding discussion highlight areas of educational need for hearing impaired children. Programs benefiting such children should include some or all of the following elements: (a) early identification, (b) parent guidance and participation, (c) concept development, (d) preschool education, (e) auditory training, (f) speech training, and (g) speechreading and/or sign language.

Early identification of the child with a hearing impairment is essential in order to initiate auditory and speech training before lack of exposure to language results in a more serious deprivation. Assistance in providing hearing and language experiences can serve to enrich the child's total fund of information and enhance his intellectual and social growth. Parents can participate directly in providing these experiences.

Development of basic social skills and exposure to a variety of experiences are essential for the hearing impaired child. Emphasis upon exposure can help foster healthy social and interpersonal relationships. It can also minimize the limitation hearing impairment places upon the amount of information that the child obtains from the environment.

Hearing impaired children need activities which contribute to conceptual development. Skills should include comparisons of sizes, shapes, and colors of objects (Evelsizer, 1972). Understanding of these concepts will increase the opportunities for meaningful experiences in which there is variety, novelty, and occasion for selection. Such experiences can contribute to development of divergent thinking and evaluation. It is in these two areas, divergent thinking and evaluation, that hearing impairment affects intelligence most directly and generally (Myklebust, 1964).

Furth (1973) suggests that development of cognition and intelligence should precede emphasis upon language under the theoretical framework that thought precedes language. Placing primary emphasis upon early identification and diagnosis, conceptual development, auditory training, and building a base of general experiences should be consistent with such a conceptualization.

It has been the experience of educators of the hearing impaired that early work on language is important to language development in the child (McConnell, 1973). The longer the deprivation, the greater the handicap. Approaches to language may include speechreading and speech training in which the child is exposed in a systematic way to oral language. One advantage of acquiring ability in speech and speechreading rather than just manual communication skills is that it enables the child to communicate with normally hearing persons.

The use of sign language in the form of manual signs or finger spelling permits the deaf child to communicate with other deaf individuals. Signs and gestures may be used when total lack of hearing, visual impairment, or reduced mental functioning render an individual unable to acquire speech and speechreading skills with reasonable facility. While some educators tend to feel that use of manual signs may retard or interfere with development of speaking and speechreading skills if introduced early (McConnell, 1973), there is some evidence that use of manualism may not interfere and perhaps may even facilitate overall language development (Alterman, 1970; Meadow, 1968; Stuckless and Birch, 1966; Vernon and Koh, 1970).

Postscript

It would be a mistake to argue that hearing impaired children are just like all other children. They are not. By virtue of their exceptionalities they are different. The personal and social success of hearing impaired children depends upon the degree to which we as individuals and as a society will accept their differences and upon the quality of methods, techniques, and devices developed to ameliorate their handicapping condition.

Ponder These

1

Think of some methods you could use to determine the possibility of a hearing loss in young children.

2

How would you teach a person, deaf from birth, the following words:

door	cut
head	vote
run	danger
fair	his own name (e.g., Ralph)
love	sex

3

Discuss the pros and cons of teaching communication skills to deaf people using the following methods:

oral communication

manual communication (e.g., signing and finger spelling)

simultaneous oral and manual communication

References

Alterman, A. I. Language and the education of children with early profound deafness. *American Annals of the Deaf,* 1970, *115,* 514–21.

Davis, H. Abnormal hearing and deafness. In H. Davis and S. R. Silverman (Eds.), *Hearing and deafness.* 3rd ed. New York: Holt, Rinehart & Winston, 1970.

Evelsizer, R. L. Hearing impairment in the young child. In A. H. Adams (Ed.), *Threshold learning abilities: diagnostic and instructional procedures for specific early learning disabilities.* New York: Macmillan, 1972.

Furth, H. G. *Deafness and learning: a psychosocial approach.* Belmont, Calif.: Wadsworth, 1973.

McConnell, F. Children with hearing disabilities. In L. M. Dunn (Ed.), *Exceptional children in the schools: special education in transition.* 2nd ed. New York: Holt, Rinehart & Winston, 1973.

McGee, T. M. Ototoxic antibiotics. *Volta Review,* 1968, *70,* 667–71.

Meadow, K. P. Early manual communication in relation to the deaf child's intellectual, social, and communicative functioning. *American Annals of the Deaf,* 1968, *113,* 29–41.

Myklebust, H. R. *The psychology of deafness: sensory deprivation, learning and adjustment.* 2nd ed. New York: Grune & Stratton, 1964.

Silverman, S. R. and H. S. Lane. Deaf children. In H. Davis and S. R. Silverman (Eds.), *Hearing and deafness.* 3rd ed. New York: Holt, Rinehart & Winston, 1970.

Streng, A., W. J. Fitch, L. D. Hedgecock, J. W. Phillips, and J. A. Carrell. *Hearing therapy for children.* 2nd ed. New York: Grune & Stratton, 1958.

Stuckless, E. R. and J. W. Birch. The influence of early manual communication on the linguistic development of deaf children. *American Annals of the Deaf,* 1966, *111,* 499–504.

U. S. Office of Education. *Estimated number of handicapped children in the United States,* 1971–72. Washington, D.C.: U. S. Office of Education, 1971.

Vernon, M. and S. D. Koh. Early manual communication and deaf children's achievement. *American Annals of the Deaf,* 1970, *115,* 527–36.

Wiley, J. A psychology of auditory impairment. In W. M. Cruickshank (Ed.), *Psychology of exceptional children and youth.* 3rd ed. Englewood Cliffs, N. J.: Prentice-Hall, 1971.

eight

Giftedness

I was standing at the front of the room explaining how the earth revolves and how, because of its huge size, it is difficult for us to realize that it is actually round. All of a sudden Spencer blurted out, "The earth isn't round." I curtly replied, "Ha, do you think it's flat?" He matter-of-factly said, "No, it's a truncated sphere." I quickly changed the subject. While the children were at recess I had a chance to grab a soft drink in the teacher's lounge. While sipping my drink, I looked up the word "truncated" in the dictionary. I'm still not sure if he was right, but it sounded good; so good that I wasn't going to make an issue of it. Spencer said the darndest things.

It was explained quite clearly to his father that Albert would never make a success of *anything*, and when Albert was expelled from the gymnasium he was emphatically told, "Your presence in the class is disruptive and affects the other students." According to Clark (1971, p. 12) Albert's last name was Einstein.

Barlow (1952), quoting from the mid-nineteenth century *Chamber's Journal,* reported the arithmetical examination given to Truman Stafford, a child prodigy. The examination was given by the Rev. H. W. Adams when Truman was ten years old.

I had only to read the sum to him once . . . . Let this fact be remembered in connection with some of the long and blind sums I shall hereafter name, and see if it does not show his amazing power of conception and comprehension. The questions given him became continually harder. What number is that which, being divided by the product of its digits, the quotient is 3; and if 18 be added, the digits will be inverted? He flew out of his chair, whirled around, rolled up his eyes and said in about a minute, 24. Multiply in your head 365,365,365,365,365,365 by 365,365,365,365,365,365. He flew around the room like a top, pulled his pantaloons over the tops of his boots, bit his hands, rolled his eyes in their sockets, sometimes smiling and talking, and then seeming to be in an agony, until, in not more than one minute said he, 133,491,850,208,566,925,016,658,299,951,583,225! (p. 43)

Mr. Palcuzzi, principal of the Jefferson Elementary School, once got tired of hearing objections to special provisions for gifted children, so he decided to spice an otherwise mild PTA meeting with *his* proposal for the gifted. The elements of the Palcuzzi program were as follows:

1. Children should be grouped by ability.
2. Part of the school day should be given over to special instruction.
3. Talented students should be allowed time to share their talents with children of other schools in the area or even of other schools throughout the state. (We will pay the transportation costs.)
4. A child should be advanced according to his talents, rather than according to his age.
5. These children should have special teachers, specially trained and highly salaried.

As might be expected, the "Palcuzzi program" was subjected to a barrage of criticism:

"What about the youngster who isn't able to fit into the special group; won't his ego be damaged?"

"How about the special cost; how could you justify transportation costs that would have to be paid by moving a special group of students from one school to another?"

"Mightn't we be endangering the child by having him interact with children who are much more mature than he is?"

"Wouldn't the other teachers complain if we gave more money to the instructors of this group?"

After listening for ten or fifteen minutes, Mr. Palcuzzi dropped his bomb! He said that he wasn't describing a *new* program for the intellectually gifted, but a program the school system had been enthusiastically supporting for a number of years — the program for *gifted basketball players!* Gallagher (1964) refers to this as the "Palcuzzi Ploy" (pp. 89–90).

The Palcuzzi Ploy illustrates the very real problem of selling the general public on differential education for the gifted. There has been a tendency to view *equal* education for all as being the *same* educational practices for all. Even though the major objective of public school education is to provide educational programs that will allow all individuals to develop to their maximum potential. When children reach some type of intellectual ceiling we tend to say, "Enough is enough! You only need to learn so much and we don't need a bunch of intellectual elitists around here anyway."

The gifted are generally perceived as being capable of shifting for themselves. In fact, many people feel that they will learn even under the most adverse learning conditions. The fact of the matter is that the gifted possess a unique array of learning characteristics that are best utilized through nontraditional teaching techniques. In other words, the learning and thinking of gifted children are best facilitated through special education services. Lindsley (1971), when talking about exceptional children, emphasized that while the retarded drop out of the bottom of the normal class the gifted pop out of the top. "Gifted and learning disabled students are retarded by the curriculum assigned them in the average classroom.

The gifted child is not stimulated to perform to his ultimate; the retarded child can't perform to the average" (p. 115).

While handicapped children can arouse sympathy and empathy, the gifted are left to fend for themselves in the regular classroom. They are capable of learning at such a high level of cognition that traditional instruction is often boring, tedious, and redundant for them. It is no wonder that many case histories of very bright individuals reveal that at some time in their lives they experienced difficulties in school. Kirk (1972) reported that Norbert Wiener, one of the great men in cybernetics, read *Alice in Wonderland* and *The Arabian Nights* by age four but was refused admission to school because he was not old enough. At age seven he was placed in the third grade. At age eighteen he received his Ph.D. in mathematics.

It is common knowledge that Albert Einstein was bored in school and maintained a below-average to mediocre school record. Thomas Edison, at the age of seven, was at the bottom of his class. His mother got so upset with the school that she pulled him out of class and taught him at home. He was never again admitted to a public school. Stories like these tend to confirm the popular belief that the gifted can and will learn on their own.

But what about the gifted child who does not make it? The talented child who drops out of school because he is bored and unchallenged? What about Dorothy J., a middle-aged Cahuilla Indian woman? In spite of Dorothy's fear of teachers and lack of knowledge of English, she completed high school. As reported by Martinson (1973), "She is co-author, with university professors, of several books in linguistics, ethnobotany, and music and has served as a university lecturer both in the United States and abroad. Meanwhile, because she lacks formal higher education, she earns a living on an assembly line in a factory near her reservation" (p. 205).

Definition

It would seem that there are as many definitions of the gifted as there are authorities in the field of giftedness. In general, "giftedness" refers to being very intelligent or highly competent in areas of academic achievement. Some authorities say you have to have an IQ of 130 or more while others say an IQ of 115 is high enough. The most recent trend in defining the gifted is to de-emphasize high IQ and emphasize creativity and specific talents, since the latter variables are believed to indicate *types* of giftedness (Getzels and Dillon, 1973).

Prevalence

As definitions change, so do the prevalence figures. That is predictable. Based on the normal curve, approximately 15 to 16 per cent of the population earn IQs of 115 or above, while only 2 to 3 per cent earn IQs of 130 or above. Because of the difficulty of assessing giftedness among children from disadvantaged cultures, Martinson (1973) has posed an interesting idea; designating the upper 3 per cent of each cultural group as gifted. Thus, different IQ cut-off limits may be selected for each cultural group. It is common knowledge that currently used intelligence tests were standardized on white middle-class populations and, thus, tend to discriminate against minority groups. Martinson's proposal allows us an opportunity to temporarily evade or by-pass the issue of culturally biased tests. The United States Office of Education estimates that 2 per cent of the school-aged population is gifted, while Marland (1972) in an influential report to the United States Congress, estimated 3 to 5 per cent. Because of the impact and influence of this document, it is safe to assume that 3 to 5 per cent is a commonly accepted prevalence figure.

Characteristics

In describing the gifted, mention must be made of Terman's monumental contribution, *Genetic Studies of Genius* (Cox, 1926; Burks, Jensen, and Terman, 1930; Terman, 1925; Terman and Oden, 1947; Terman and Oden, 1959). Terman actually devoted his life to the study of 1,528 gifted children, and he followed them thirty-five years from 1920 to his death in 1956. This five-volume study is expected to continue to the year 2010. The study is not only noted for its large sample size and longitudinal contribution, but for its consistent accuracy. The findings of Terman's investigation have been confirmed and reconfirmed to the point of "bordering on redundancy" (Getzels and Dillon, 1973, p. 694).

Basically, Terman's study counteracts the mythical concept that gifted individuals are physically weak, small in stature, wear glasses, read all the time, are not interesting to be around, and are "book-wormish." Terman's findings indicate that not only are the gifted superior in intellect, but that they also are physically, socially, emotionally, and morally advanced. Terman's gifted subjects, were reported to be taller, stronger, and heavier than nongifted children. They walked earlier and had a lower incidence of sensory defects, malnutrition, and poor posture. They came from above-average to high-income homes, and their parents were well educated. When compared with the general population, they had a low incidence of delinquency, mental illness, and alcoholism. The gifted seemed to be more happily married, to have fewer divorces, and to have fewer offspring. Of over 1,500 offspring, there is a reported mean IQ of 132, with only 2 per cent falling below 100 and 33⅓ per cent scoring over 140. After studying Terman's classic work you cannot help but wonder what causes giftedness.

Etiology

Galton's (1869) classic contribution to the quantitative psychological study of giftedness touched off the nature-nurture controversy. His examination of adult geniuses lent support to the argument for a hereditary cause. In the years after his study, environmental aspects were accentuated by the majority of authorities in the field of the gifted. However, it was observed that gifted individuals walked, talked, and read much earlier than "normals," and such early acceleration in behavioral development was difficult to attribute primarily to environmental events. Yet it was also observed that the environments in which the majority of the gifted developed were unquestionably wholesome and stimulating. Since the nature-nurture controversy became so complex and conjured up emotional overtones, a pragmatic resolution evolved: "We are unable to genetically manipulate variables by selective breeding, but we are able to manipulate environmental events that may facilitate intellectual growth." This practical approach is best summed up by Gallagher (1964):

> Environment can have either an inhibiting or encouraging effect on the development of intellectual talent. Such an assumption places a heavy responsibility on the culture and its educational system, but it is also an exciting one for the educator and social

scientist. The concept of *intelligence* as a genetically determined trait has been replaced by the concept of a pliable and plastic intellect which is responsible to the environment in which it is placed. The place of genetics and intelligence has not been denied; rather, the place of environment in its interaction with genetics has been reaffirmed (p. 20).

While the logic of this approach seems irrefutable, Jensen (1966, 1969) insisted that genes and prenatal development accounts for 80 per cent of the variance in intelligence while only 20 per cent of the variance can be accounted for by the environment. Citing research studies, growth figures, and models of intelligence, Jensen presented a convincing case. Torrance (1971) summarizes Jensen's position as follows:

He especially questioned the idea that IQ differences are almost entirely a result of environmental differences and the cultural bias of intelligence tests. As in his earlier papers, he argued that environmental factors are less important in determining IQ than genetic factors. After examining the recent research concerning compensatory educational programs for young children, Jensen concluded that extreme environmental deprivation can keep a child from performing up to his genetic potential, but an enriched educational program cannot push the child above that potential. Jensen argues, however, that there are other mental abilities not included in intelligence tests that might be capitalized upon in educational programs. He believes that current educational attempts to boost IQ have been misdirected, and he advocates the development of educational methods that are based on other mental abilities besides IQ (p. 550).

Creativity

Another classic work on the gifted is Getzels and Jackson's (1962) study of the relationship between IQ and creativity. Two groups were identified: (a) high on IQ and low on creativity (mean IQ 150) and (b) low on IQ and high on creativity (mean IQ 127). High IQ-low creativity was defined as the top 20 per cent on IQ but low on creative thinking: low IQ-high creativity was defined as the top 20 per cent on creativity but lower on IQ. Despite a 23-point difference in IQ, both groups performed equally well on standardized achievement tests. The major finding was that while creativity may be a facet of intelligence, it is not being measured by the typical standardized intelligence tests. Apparently, creativity is not being tapped by conventional methods of measurement and evaluation.

Since there exists a low tolerance for nonconformity in our society, and creativity is often discouraged, Torrance (1965) attempted to accelerate creativeness in children by offering them two-dollar prizes for stories that were interesting, exciting, and unusual. He found that children would produce such stories when reinforced for doing so. Torrance and others have demonstrated that creative thinking abilities need to be energized and guided, and that the earlier this is done the better.

Differential Education

As listed by Ward (1962), the logic of special education services for the gifted is based on the following assumptions and observed facts:

(1)   Gifted children as a group differ from others in learning ability; they learn faster and remember more, and they tend to think more deeply with and about what they learn.

(2)   As adults, gifted persons tend to remain similarly advanced beyond the average and tend to assume distinctive social roles as leaders in the reconstruction and advancement of whatever lines of activity they engage in.

(3)   The regular school curriculum only barely approximates the demands of either the greater learning capacity or the anticipated social roles of gifted persons.

(4)   An educational program *can* be devised which *does* more adequately meet these basic demands, and which on the whole being uniquely suited to the gifted is both unnecessary for and impossible of accomplishment by students of lesser ability.

(5)   Differential educational provisions for the gifted promise to discover more gifted persons, to improve their education, and to launch them earlier into their chosen careers so that society, as well as the persons themselves, may enjoy longer the fruits of their productive and creative labors (p. 22).

As a result of the need for differential education, three basic administrative approaches for providing special services have been developed. They are (a) enrichment, (b) ability grouping, and (c) acceleration.

Enrichment. Referring to some adaptation of the regular educational program, enrichment usually implies that the gifted are not to be separated from their normal peers. Enrichment is of two kinds: (a) horizontal and (b) vertical. Horizontal enrichment refers to providing *more* educational experiences at the same level of difficulty, while vertical enrichment refers to providing higher-level activities of increasing complexity. Although the majority of gifted students in special education are involved in enrichment-type programs, there is little evidence to support their efficacy.

Ability grouping. In this method the gifted are separated into more homogeneous groupings through special classes, ability tracks, and so forth. Although the results of research on ability grouping are somewhat contradictory, there is sufficient evidence that the gifted benefit from such programs to provoke further investigation. Getzels and Dillon (1973) quote Gold as saying, "Grouping apparently is a helpful but not automatically effective instructional adjustment; achievement seems to improve only when grouping is accompanied by a differentiation in teacher quality, curriculum, guidance and method" (p. 716).

Acceleration. By this means the student is moved through the traditional program at a faster rate or begins his education earlier. Gifted children may enter school early, skip grades, go to summer school, earn college credit in high school, and the like. Research seems clearly to support acceleration, but programs of this type meet with criticism and disfavor. "Apparently the cultural values favoring a standard period of dependency and formal education are stronger than the social or individual need for achievement and independence. This is an instance of the more general case one remarks throughout education: when research findings clash with cultural values, the values are more likely to prevail" (Getzels and Dillon, 1973, p. 717).

Although administrative arrangements for handling any student — handicapped, normal, or gifted — *assist* or interfere with instruction, the crux of education centers around what goes on in the classroom. No administrative manipulation of environmental variables can *assure* learning. This is not to minimize the importance of administrative approaches, but it is commonly recognized that although appropriate facilities, materials, and wholesome environmental conditions assist the teacher in his job, these important facets are no substitute for a conscientious, sensitive, skillful, and competent teacher.

Conclusion

Gifted students are very bright, yet they, too, need attention and selected stimulation, and their learning and thinking can most certainly be inhibited or suppressed. If we are to do what we say *should* be done, that is, develop each individual to his optimum or maximum potential, then we must take another look at our educational services for the gifted.

Not only is differential instruction important to the gifted individual himself, it may very well be important to society. We are living in a world that grows more complex every day. War, crime, drugs, alcoholism, overpopulation, and pollution are problems that threaten our very survival. How may these problems be resolved? It just may be that we will have to turn to the gifted and hope they can come up with some answers.

In the 1950s, during the era of Sputnik, the nation turned to the gifted for solutions to problems in the physical sciences as they pertained to space exploration. The public at that time supported differential educational programs for the gifted, especially those programs relating to science. Unfortunately, the programs were short-lived, as the United States quickly caught up in the space race. At present, it is the social sciences that need a booster shot. We should begin now to train our gifted individuals and entice them into the area of social science exploration.

Maslow's (1971) analogy of how tall man can grow and how fast man can run, brings the value and importance of the gifted into meaningful perspective: [1]

> If we want to answer the question how tall can the human species grow, then obviously it is well to pick out the ones who are already tallest and study them. If we want to know how fast a human being can run, then it is no use to average out the speed of a "good sample" of the population, it is far better to collect Olympic gold-medal winners and see how well they can do. If we want to know the possibilities for spiritual growth,

---

[1] From Maslow, A., *The Farther Reaches of Human Nature,* Copyright © 1971 by Bertha G. Maslow, p. 7. Reprinted by permission of The Viking Press, Inc., New York.

value growth, or moral development in human beings, then I maintain that we can learn most by studying our most moral, ethical, or saintly people.

On the whole I think it fair to say that human history is a record of the ways in which human nature has been sold short. The highest possibilities of human nature have practically always been underrated. Even when "good specimens," the saints and sages and great leaders of history, have been available for study, the temptation too often has been to consider them not human but supernaturally endowed (p. 7).

As we begin to think about the gifted as a human resource to solve society's problems, we must be aware that we have no right to harness their intellectual talents at the cost of their basic freedoms. Getzels (1957) reminds us that there comes a time when we must look at the gifted as people and not be compelled to figure out how we can get the most out of them. Hopefully, if they are properly treated in our educational settings, gifted persons will find gratification as well as intriguing challenges in all learning.

Ponder These

1

By what criteria could the following individuals be judged to be gifted?

Richard M. Nixon   Alfred E. Newman

Henry Kissinger   Hugh Hefner

Thomas Jefferson   Lee Harvey Oswald

Jimmy Durante   Lester Maddox

Adolf Hitler   Marilyn Monroe

Is it possible to become nationally known — a household word — without being gifted?

2

Read some accounts, factual or fictional, of giftedness (for example, *The Child Buyer*, by Lewis Hersey or *Mental Prodigies*, by Fred Barlow). How would you handle a child described in the accounts in a regular public school class?

3

Plan a hypothetical educational program to *make* children gifted. Would the opposite of your program *make* children retarded?

References

Barlow, F. *Mental prodigies*. New York: Greenwood Press, 1952.

Burks, B., D. Jensen, and L. M. Terman. The promise of youth. *Genetic studies of genius*. Vol. 3. Stanford, Calif.: Stanford University Press, 1930.

Clark, R. W. *Einstein. The life and times*. New York: World, 1971.

Cox, C. M. The early mental traits of 300 geniuses. *Genetic studies of genius*. Vol. 2. Stanford, Calif.: Stanford University Press, 1926.

Gallagher, J. J. *Teaching the gifted child*. Boston: Allyn & Bacon, 1964.

Galton, F. *Hereditary genius: An inquiry into its laws and consequences*. London: Macmillan, 1869.

Getzels, J. W. Social values and individual motives: The dilemma of the gifted. *School Review*, 1957, *65*, 60–63.

Getzels, J. W. and J. T. Dillon. The nature of giftedness and the education of the gifted. In R. M. W. Travers (Ed.), *Second handbook of research on teaching*. Chicago: Rand McNally, 1973.

Getzels, J. W. and P. W. Jackson. *Creativity and intelligence: Explorations with gifted students*. New York: Wiley, 1962.

Jensen, A. R. How much can we boost IQ and scholastic achievement? *Harvard Educational Review*, 1969, *39*, 1–119.

Jensen, A. R. Verbal mediation and educational potential. *Psychology in the Schools*, 1966, *3*, 99–109.

Kirk, S. A. *Educating exceptional children*. Rev. ed. Boston: Houghton Mifflin, 1972.

Lindsley, O. R. Precision teaching in perspective: An interview with Ogden R. Lindsley. *Teaching Exceptional Children*, 1971, *31*, 114–19.

Marland, S. P. *Education of the gifted and talented*. Washington, D.C.: U.S. Office of Education, 1972.

Martinson, R. A. Children with superior cognitive abilities. In L. M. Dunn (Ed.), *Exceptional children in the schools*, Rev. ed. New York: Holt, Rinehart & Winston, 1973.

Maslow, A. H. *The farther reaches of human nature*. New York: Viking Press, 1971.

Terman, L. M. Mental and physical traits of a thousand gifted children. *Genetic studies of genius*. Vol. 1. Stanford, Calif: Stanford University Press, 1925.

Terman, L. M. and M. H. Oden. The gifted child grows up. *Genetic studies of genius.* Vol. 4. Stanford, Calif.: Stanford University Press, 1947.

Terman, L. M. and M. H. Oden. The gifted group at mid-life. *Genetic studies of genius.* Vol. 5. Stanford, Calif.: Stanford University Press, 1959.

Torrance, E. P. Psychology of gifted children and youth. In W. M. Cruickshank (Ed.), *Psychology of exceptional children and youth.* 3rd ed. Englewood Cliffs, N.J.: Prentice-Hall, 1971.

Torrance, E. P. *Rewarding creative behavior: Experiments in classroom creativity.* Englewood Cliffs, N.J.: Prentice-Hall, 1965.

Ward, V. S. (Ed.) *The gifted student: A manual for program improvement.* Charlottesville, Va.: Southern Regional Education Board, 1962.

nine

Early Childhood

Darrell was the kind of preschooler every teacher dreads having in the class — a four-year-old public nuisance. Unable (or unwilling) to follow the simplest directions, he could usually be found poking an innocent classmate or doing his best in any number of ways to disrupt my Head Start class. But Darrell was not incapable of showing affection. I cannot easily forget the day he interrupted his finger painting to "lovingly" hug me and run his paint-covered fingers through my hair. I thought I caught a devilish gleam in his eye when he released his grip, but I quickly dismissed it. Darrell had long been tagged M.R. and his misbehavior, we all knew, was due to his mental disability. Thus, Darrell was forgiven for this and other equally trying acts in the classroom.

It was George Washington's birthday, and I stood the class in a circle and put on a favorite record, "Chopping Down the Cherry Tree." The record was ideal for gross-motor development. I instructed the children to swing their arms rhythmically to the "chop chop" of the music as if they were all little Georges chopping away at the proverbial cherry tree. The children loved it. Everyone swung his imaginary ax with the greatest enthusiasm — everyone of course except "dumb" Darrell who just stood there with his arms straight out in front of him, hands clasped together making a huge fist. Patiently I attempted to teach Darrell the act of chopping. But even after much demonstrating and coaxing, he stubbornly refused to change his original position and continued to stand motionless with his "ax" extended. Close to the end of my patience, I cried, "Darrell why won't you chop with your ax like the rest of us?" The reply shocked me into reassessing Darrell's M.R. label: "I don't need to chop. Can't you see I have a power saw!"[1]

Placed in a strange environment, the one thing that preschoolers are not is predictable. Thus, I prepared myself for the worst when I took my Head Start class of thirty inner-city four-year-olds to the famous Bronx Zoo. How could I expect them to be orderly and restrained? Flashing through my mind were frightful fantasies of Freddy taking a bath with the walruses or Linda slipping through the bars to pet the leopards. To my great surprise, the children were very well behaved despite their obvious excitement at viewing the many wild animals which previously had been only magazine pictures to them. My only major problem in controlling the children occurred quite unexpectedly as we rounded a corner and faced a large square of lush green grass bearing several "Keep off the grass" signs. After having survived elephant pens and monkey cages, I was hardly concerned about a grassy plot of ground. I was, in fact, stunned when almost every child bolted from our orderly little procession and tumbled onto the grass screaming with delight. It took me several seconds to realize that these unfortunate inner-city children were growing up playing on concrete sidewalks and streets of black asphalt and broken glass. That simple plot of green grass gave them their greatest thrill of our entire zoo trip.

Craig was the precocious one of the group. I was continually in awe of his insight and his eagerness to solve the mysteries of

---

[1]We are grateful to Ms. Roxana G. Davison for contributing this anecdote.

his world. Of course, there were a few times when even Craig put two and two together and mistakenly came up with five.

Craig's mother, a divorcee, was dating an obstetrician. Like so many preschoolers, Craig kept his teachers and classmates well informed about his mother's personal life by frequently making announcements such as, "My mother dates a doctor named Phil, and he delivers real babies."

One day as we were out for a drive, Craig shouted, "Oh, look! There's Dr. Phil's house!" Pointing to a van parked in front of the house, he said, "There's his truck too!" Since I was acquainted with Dr. Phil and knew that he owned no truck, I said gently, "No, Craig, that truck doesn't belong to Dr. Phil." Looking me squarely in the eyes, he impatiently retorted, "Well, I bet it is too his truck. He _must_ have a truck because Mommy says he _delivers_ babies!"

Rationale for Early Childhood Education

Early scholars such as Montessori, Froebel, and Hall first directed attention toward early childhood as important foundation years for learning. A widespread interest in early childhood education, however, did not develop until the 1960s when psychological research began to reveal that the early years are indeed most critical for a child's future development.

Research findings suggest that the rate of a child's learning roughly parallels that of his physical growth. It appears that learning occurs quite rapidly in the first two years, slightly less rapidly for the next four, and then begins to level off to a lower and gradually decreasing rate. In fact, Benjamin Bloom (1964) asserts that by age four a child has already developed 50 per cent of his total intellectual capacity. And by age eight he has attained 80 per cent of his capacity. Skeel's (1966) important study of orphanage children dramatically demonstrates that modifying a child's environment during the early formative years can greatly improve his capacity for intellectual and social development at a later age.

Today a sound foundation during the early childhood years is considered essential for subsequent success in school. The need for adequate early experiences is most crucial for those children suffering from physical, emotional, mental, or social handicaps. Provided early with special educational services, handicapped children can often overcome or learn to cope with their difficulties and, in many cases, can successfully progress through public school with their peers.

In past years the advice given to parents of exceptional children by physicians, teachers, and psychologists was often ill-founded: "Just wait and see what happens. He'll probably grow out of it." Unfortunately, very few children did "grow out of it." Instead, difficulties were compounded and they fell further and further behind their nonhandicapped peers. Experts now realize that delivery of special educational services early in a child's life not only can prevent school failure but may well relieve taxpayers of the high cost of providing years of remedial educational services or lifetime economic assistance to the handicapped individual. Thus, both psychoeducational and economic concerns recommend the employment of special educational programs in the early childhood years.

Definition of Early Childhood Education

Early childhood education was traditionally conceived of as the group learning experiences provided for children from the ages of three to eight. Thus, programs for early childhood education encompassed nursery schools, kindergartens, and primary grades. The growing realization, however, that infancy and toddlerhood are critical years for later social and intellectual development has largely accounted for the current notion that early childhood education embraces programs for all children under nine years of age. Quite logically, a significant proportion of educational and psychological research is now focused on the infant and toddler years.

Prevalence of Young Handicapped Children

Although exact incidence figures are unavailable, it is estimated that approximately one million preschool children in the United States suffer from physical, emotional, and mental handicaps. Of those children identifiable as in need of special services, many are multiply handicapped, having secondary deficits accompanying their major disability. Most of the young exceptional children do not fit neatly into the traditional special education compartments. For instance, a mentally retarded child may have a speech problem compounded by emotional difficulties or poor vision. Thus, incidence figures for each area of exceptionality fail to reveal the magnitude of the educational difficulties confronting teachers. Unfortunately, due to the shortage of adequately trained personnel and insufficient funds, only a small percentage of the young special children are receiving the educational experiences necessary to insure them later successful school adjustment.

Etiology

The causes of disabilities in young children comprise five major categories: (a) genetic, (b) prenatal, (c) perinatal, (d) postnatal, and (e) cultural. Since a child's difficulty often results from a complex interaction of two or more factors, many educators focus attention on remediation rather than search for causes. However, remediation can sometimes be facilitated when etiological factors are understood.

Genetic difficulties include biochemical disorders, such as galactosemia and phenylketonuria (PKU), and such chromosomal abnormalities as Down's syndrome (mongolism). Today both PKU and galactosemia can be detected by urine tests, and if found early the harmful effects can be reversed by putting the infant on special diets. Some prenatal conditions frequently associated with childhood disabilities are (a) prenatal anoxia, from premature separation of the placenta, severe anemia, or a heart condition of the mother, (b) the Rh factor, and (c) rubella contracted by the mother during the first trimester of pregnancy. Birth injuries, asphyxia, and prematurity are among the perinatal conditions which may affect the child during or immediately preceding birth. During infancy and early childhood, handicapping conditions can result from malnutrition, accidental physical trauma (especially to the brain), and from diseases and infections such as encephalitis, meningitis, and chronic otitus media. Finally, it appears that a great proportion of the children suffering from school learning difficulties have simply not received the necessary cultural prerequisites such as social and educational stimulation.

Potentially handicapping conditions which affect the growing organism early in life generally exert a more detrimental influence that those occurring in later stages of development. An expectant mother (already a developed organism) suffering from malnutrition or rubella usually does not experience the severe and lasting impairment to which her fetus is so susceptible. Moreover, rubella usually produces a more profound abnormality in the fetus when contracted in the first month of pregnancy than in the third month. Similarly, malnutrition and environmental deficiencies affect a child more severely when experienced during the first rather than during the fifth year of life. Obviously satisfaction of the child's early medical, nutritional, social, and educational needs is essential to maximize his opportunities for healthy development. And it is equally true that the sooner an etiological factor is arrested or ameliorated, the less profound will be its debilitating effects. Unfortunately, early delivery of services which may be of great importance to some young children and their families is frequently difficult. Not only are funds and services limited, but the identification of children with potential handicapping conditions is no easy task.

Early Identification

As efforts to provide additional health and educational services for young children are stepped up, it becomes increasingly crucial that teachers begin to assume an active role in identifying those children likely to benefit most from these services. Although some conditions are immediately obvious, other more subtle and difficult to detect problems are often present. Developmental lags or deviations in children are frequently overlooked because parents lack basic knowledge in child development and have little opportunity to compare their child's development with that of his peers. (Allen, Rieke, Dmitriev, and Hayden, 1972). Moreover, even those few parents who can quickly detect minor disabilities in other children, are often oblivious to their own child's slight limp, speech delay, or vision impairment. Understandably, most parents find it difficult to admit that their child is handicapped.

By failing to acknowledge a child's disability, parents can at least temporarily avoid the stark realization that remediation may require years of work and patience. Such reality-avoidance often prevents the handicapped child from receiving professional attention in the early years when remediation is easier. And this unfortunate fact underscores the importance of the teacher's role in identifying handicaps.

Teachers should proceed with considerable caution, however, in their efforts to avail disabled children of needed services. Their job should be simply to observe the children carefully and alert parents that additional help *may* be needed. Teachers must remember that they are not in a position to render a definitive diagnosis of a disorder, except an educational disorder.

Before causing parents needless alarm, the teacher should recognize that whether or not a particular developmental skill is appropriate may depend on the community in which the child lives, and that personal judgments of disability may be subject to cultural or educational bias. Branding a child as handicapped can have devastating effects on his self-esteem, and the label may well become a self-fulfilling prophecy. Stated differently, low expectations can encourage low performance.

Clearly, it is within the teacher's proper role to observe the children carefully and to obtain professional assistance in interpreting behavioral signs. Appropriate parental warnings and referrals for further diagnosis should be made only after the teacher systematically records observations of the child's behavior. Every early childhood teacher should familiarize himself with developmental, age-appropriate behaviors and with potentially troublesome behaviors in young children. The teacher should keep in mind that even among "normal" children vast differences abound in the physical, social, and intellectual growth rates of individuals. Only those children who after careful observation appear well behind their peers in some basic facet of development will need to be referred for further diagnosis and special services. (For lists of specific behaviors indicative of potential problems, see Allen, Rieke, Dmitriev, and Hayden, 1972, and Wallace and Kauffman, 1973.)

Language Development

That language and intellectual competence are closely intertwined is becoming increasingly obvious. Often accompanying immature language are such immature thought processes as delayed discrimination and reasoning skills. Indeed severe language delay or inadequacy is the most significant single behavioral sign indicating a young child's need for special help in order to succeed in school.

Socialization depends upon experiences with language and communication. The ability to abstract the essence of experiences and the urge and power to express complex thoughts and feelings is uniquely human. Although animals may respond to symbols for specific things, such as a dog knowing he is going for a walk when he sees his leash, only man can generalize from his experiences and share his analysis and synthesis of ideas with others. From infancy on, man's learning is dependent upon his acquisition of the communication code of his culture.

The very young child faces the task of learning to understand the confusing happenings in his world. In early childhood his understanding is restricted to the immediate and concrete. Concomitant with the development of his language skills, he gradually begins to deal with abstractions and his symbolization becomes increasingly complex.

Unfortunately, as all educators know, the path leading from simple and concrete communication to the complex and abstract variety of understanding is a treacherous one that can be followed only if the child is afforded the appropriate environmental experiences. He must have a rich and stimulating language environment in his early childhood years if he is to develop verbal skills essential for later school success. Moreover, if a child is to develop his intellect and expressive skills, he must be provided with stimulating sensory and social experiences which involve him emotionally and help create a need for communication. Clearly insufficient and unsatisfying experiences with the social and physical worlds can hamper a child's drive to talk and question. They may eventually reduce his motivation and create language patterns which cause school failure.

The language patterns of many children from lower socioeconomic levels have recently emerged as a source of considerable concern to linguists, psychologist, and educators. The language of lower-class children often differs significantly from the standard English spoken by middle-class children and teachers within the public schools. Bereiter and Engelmann (1966) go so far as to equate cultural deprivation with language deprivation, insisting that if the lower-class child is to succeed in school he must learn the middle-class language of the school system. Similarly, Bloom (1965) treats the speech of lower-class children in terms of "language deficit." He maintains that a lower-class child's language and future learning are inhibited because his parents are less likely to provide the quantity and quality of verbal "corrective feedback" found in typical middle-class environments. Unfortunately, viewing the child from a language-deficit perspective tends to imply, quite incorrectly, that the child is deprived of a structurally systematic and functionally adequate language. Further, it suggests that the lower-class child is generally deprived of culturalization when, in fact, the deprivation relates only to middle-class culture. Hence, perceiving the lower-class child as having "language differences" rather than "language deficiencies" may be preferable (Baratz, 1969).

Whether viewed as different or deficient, the language used by a lower-class child in his home varies considerably from that which he uses in school. Hess and Shipman (1967) conducted class-related research which found language learning and intellectual growth to be by-products of the verbal interaction between mother and child. Their research revealed that middle-class mothers most often employed a democratic type of control, used expanded sentences, and provided labels for objects. Most lower-class mothers, on the other hand, used an imperative type of control, spoke in a restricted form of language, and failed to provide the child with labels for objects. Although language style does vary within lower socioeconomic groups, the lower-class child typically develops a mode of communication, perhaps adequate at home, which none-theless hinders his progress in school.

Language difficulties, however, are not unique to lower-class youngsters. Many middle- and upper-class parents fail to provide their children with a language environment conducive to later school success. Moreover, language disabilities result not only from faulty learning, but often from emotional disturbance, hearing impairment, central nervous system dysfunction, and mental retardation, none of which know social-class distinctions. Because large numbers of children within the lower class have experienced school difficulties, however, the nation's first comprehensive effort to provide prerequisite educational opportunities focused on economically disadvantaged children. Within this population were found the highest incidence not only of language differences, but also of all other types of handicaps.

Project Head Start

The first nationwide program specifically designed for children likely to experience later educational difficulties was Project Head Start. Head Start programs began with the hope of providing not only rich language environments, but also a wide range of health, nutritional, and educational experiences for the economically disadvantaged early childhood population.

The commencement of Project Head Start in the spring of 1965 engendered hope in some circles of some day ridding society of personal failure and poverty. Born under the auspices of the Office of Economic Opportunity, Project Head Start authorized the organization and establishment of six-week summer programs for children whose family income fell below the poverty level set by Congress. Geared to the early childhood years, the program attempted to provide whatever environmental supplements were needed to prevent failure in the elementary grades. Following the first summer's operation, Head Start programs for the full academic year were initiated. Although the personnel of early Head Start centers were left free to determine specific objectives and their means of achievement, greater levels of program specificity were gradually introduced.

Seven broad objectives guided the national Head Start program (Grotberg, 1969):

1. Improving the child's physical health and physical abilities;
2. Helping the emotional and social development of the child by encouraging self-confidence, spontaneity, curiosity, and self-discipline;
3. Improving the child's mental processes and skills with particular attention to conceptual and verbal skills;
4. Establishing patterns and expectations of success for the child which will create a climate of confidence for his future learning efforts;
5. Increasing the child's capacity to relate positively to family members and others while at the same time strengthening the family's ability to relate positively to his problems;
6. Developing in the child and his family a responsible attitude toward society, and fostering constructive opportunities for society to work together with the poor in solving their problems;
7. Increasing the sense of dignity and self-worth within the child and his family.

Prepared by a panel of child-development authorities, these broad objectives offered considerable latitude in decisions concerning specific activities to be undertaken in a particular Head Start center. And because of abundant differences in beliefs among centers as to the needs of children, substantial variation in programs developed. The creators of some programs emphasized development of social skills, while others concentrated on the development of good health and dietary habits. Many programs resembled a traditional nursery school, but several emphasized intensive directive instruction in language, reading-readiness skills, science, and math. In any event, the likelihood was slim that any two programs would be the same.

One of the most innovative and exciting aspects of Project Head Start was its concept of parent involvement. Actively participating parents can add continuity to the child's home and school experiences while also encouraging at-home practice of the cognitive skills which disadvantaged children may lack. In addition, a parent's active contribution to the child's education often engenders new feelings of adequacy and self-worth in the parent which in turn may enhance affectional relationships in the home (Evans, 1971).

Although federal Head Start officials encouraged parent participation they failed to adequately specify *how* parents were to be involved. Once again, there was substantial variation from center to center in this regard.

The nationwide interest in early childhood education and the exciting possibilities presented by Project Head Start appear in retrospect to have generated some unfortunate side effects. Amid the excitement, child-development experts failed to caution the nation that a six-week summer session or even a full-year program prior to school entrance would provide only a beginning in meeting the educational needs of young children. Nor did specialists adequately apprise the public that the scientific study of child development, in its infancy, could provide only a few clues about the necessary social and educational experiences required for optimal development of young children. Thus, expectations of success for Head Start ran unrealistically high.

First results of the initial research to determine Head Start's effectiveness proved promising: IQ gains were found for children participating in the original summer program. Much to everyone's disappointment, however, when the Head Start children were compared to a control group at midsemester, the gains appeared to have dissipated entirely. Finally, in 1969, the results of the Westinghouse study, largest of the Head Start evaluations, were released. Again the results proved somewhat discouraging. Head Start children did tend to score higher than controls on cognitive measures, especially those children from the southeastern geographical region and from large urban areas (Caldwell, 1972; Payne, Mercer, Payne, and Davison, 1973). But although differences were statistically significant in some localities, their magnitude was smaller than expected.

Some time after the initiation of Head Start, but even before release of the Westinghouse report, the nation's attitude toward early intervention became perceptibly more skeptical and disillusionment apparently displaced the former climate of optimism. Although Head Start had doubtless helped many young children overcome classroom difficulties, it failed to realize its promise of healing the nation's educational ills.

In many primary schools throughout the nation, Project Follow Through has been implemented as a means of sustaining early gains produced by Head Start experiences. Authorized in 1968 under the Office of Economic Opportunity, the programs provide continued educational enrichment for primary-grade children formerly enrolled in Head Start classes. Clearly, all special services for young children have the greatest chance for lasting success when continued assistance is provided in the elementary grades.

The field of early childhood education is currently experiencing a period of recovery and consolidation (Caldwell, 1972). Now, the question is not *whether* early intervention can affect children, but how and with which children we should intervene. In the brief period since the inception of Head Start, numerous psychological and educational research findings have significantly advanced our understanding of child development. Yet the kinds of experiences required by young children for optimal development remain the subject of intense debate. Rather than offering definitive solutions, the research has raised still more questions and has fanned the flames of controversy. Such effects, however, are the inevitable product of vigorous and honest research and should not discourage its continuance.

Current Trends in Early Childhood Programs

Today educational strategies for the early childhood years abound. Although a full discussion of the approaches currently in use is beyond the scope of this book, there are two major movements with which each student of early childhood education should become familiar. At the foundation of each of these approaches is a theoretical base wrought from years of psychological research. Because a grasp of underlying theoretical structure is required before a teacher can intelligently choose among approaches, the following discussion provides a very general overview of (a) Piagetian theory, which is currently influencing the British infant-school and open-school movements, and (b) the directive teaching approach based on behavior principles, derived largely from the work of Skinner (cf. Skinner, 1953).

PIAGET'S THEORY OF COGNITIVE DEVELOPMENT AND "OPEN" EDUCATION

As the child grows older, he passes through a number of progressively more mature and complex stages of thinking and learning. Following an orderly sequence, the progression is influenced by the interaction of neurological maturation with physical and social experience. Most important, the progression is affected by motivation or what Piaget calls *equilibration*. Equilibration occurs when a child seeks to reconcile new learnings with old to achieve cognitive congruence or stability. As the child assimilates and accommodates to new learnings he develops a progressively more mature cognitive structure.

According to Piaget (cf. Baldwin, 1967; Piaget, 1952) all children move through the following stages of development:

1. The *sensorimotor* period, beginning at birth and lasting through the first two years of life. During this time the child learns by rubbing, hitting, touching, and biting. He learns by interacting with the physical environment. Through his senses and movements he learns about causality, object permanence, location, time, and some of the properties of space.

2. The *preoperational* stage, occurring between the ages of two and seven. During this period the child's thinking is largely egocentric. He assumes that everyone thinks as he does and understands him without his having to explain his thoughts. He is unable to firmly grasp two ideas simultaneously or to see parts of objects in relationship to the whole. In the last part of this period the child makes intuitive judgments about relationships and begins to think in symbols. Language becomes an increasingly important way of representing the concrete world. His learning and thinking are dominated largely by perception.

3. The period of *concrete operations*, occurring between the ages of seven and eleven. During this phase the child can

see an event from different perspectives. He can order his experiences into an organized whole, but the mental activity still is dependent upon perception of concrete objects that he has manipulated.

4. The period of *formal operations,* occurring between the ages of eleven and fifteen. At this time the child's cognition begins to rely upon pure symbolism rather than upon the concrete world. He enters the world of ideas and abstractions and he uses thought to direct his observations.

Most important to Piaget's theory is the notion that each stage forms the foundation for later stages. All abstractions are based upon former experiential understanding. Attempts to teach abstract concepts without enabling the child to progress through preliminary stages will end in failure or, at best, inadequate learning. Piaget considers experience with the concrete world and ample opportunity to stabilize behavior and thought at each stage essential to the development of formal operations.

As stated by Evans (1971), the teaching approach based on Piagetian theory emphasizes

(1) active, self-discovery, inductively oriented learning experiences whereby a child is able to perform transformations on materials from the environment (where direct teaching is necessary, it follows rather than precedes periods of manipulation and exploration); (2) arrangements of moderately novel experiences which capitalize upon and facilitate stage-relevant thinking operations but simultaneously accommodate to the child's present intellectual style; (3) a variety of patterned and enriched concrete sensory experiences; (4) the symbolization of manipulative, play and aesthetic experiences; (5) provision of a variety of models for imitative learning; (6) a high rate of interpersonal interaction among children with ample opportunity for role playing, a sharing of different viewpoints, and corrective discussions led by adults under appropriate circumstances; and (7) the use of the clinical method to study children's progress (specifically for the purpose of noting the process through which a child may go en route to a problem solution) (p. 235).

There has been increasing interest in Piagetian theory among those in "informal education." Certainly, Piaget's notions of cognitive development are compatible with the approaches of the British infant school and the open classroom of the United States. In fact, wide acceptance today of these two approaches is largely attributable to the popularity which Piaget presently enjoys.

SKINNER'S BEHAVIOR PRINCIPLES AND DIRECTIVE TEACHING

Another popularly acclaimed approach to teaching in current use is derived from Skinner's (1953) behavioristic principles of learning. Behaviorists, insisting that behaviors can be taught directly, concern themselves with changing environmental consequences in order to bring about changes in students' responses. Directive teachers emphasize clearly stated lesson objectives, an orderly sequential arrangement of tasks, and positive reinforcement for correct responses. Proponents of a directive approach argue that only through provision of precise programs for children can teachers develop essential academic and social responses.

Most popular among the directive approaches to early childhood education is the Bereiter-Engelmann (1966) program. It was designed specifically for disadvantaged children, in the belief that only through directive instruction can the language and thought development of such children be accelerated quickly enough to meet the eventual demands of public schools. The Bereiter-Engelmann program led to the preparation by Engelmann and Becker of DISTAR[2]—a packaged set of instructional materials with daily lesson plans covering language, reading, and arithmetic learning.

Conclusion

Regardless of which teaching approach is used, psychological research clearly indicates that lower teacher-child ratios are likely to enhance a child's emotional and intellectual development. We have no substantial evidence, however, to indicate that any one teaching approach is superior in every situation and with every child. We do know that some exceptional children require positive reinforcement and direct instruction before they begin to manipulate and meaningfully interact with the physical environment. On the other hand, many young children clearly respond to directive teaching with greater enthusiasm and more correct responses if first given the opportunity to manipulate concrete objects. The likelihood is

[2]DISTAR is marketed by Science Research Associates.

that the young handicapped child's optimum development is best fostered in an environment which provides ample opportunity for self-directed exploration supplemented by directive instruction in his areas of greatest deficit.

No single theory is so comprehensive that it can adequately explain all language, emotional, social, and intellectual behaviors. At this time the needs of most exceptional children can best be served by drawing upon the strengths of various theories and by searching for ways to harmoniously combine approaches.

Despite difficulties in determining appropriate early school experiences, we should not despair of our efforts to meet the needs of young exceptional children. The study of human behavior is still in its infancy. Seventy years ago Freud and Watson were only beginning their studies on the nature of behavior and learning. The real impetus for early childhood education began as late as the 1960s, and we have learned much in a very short time. With continued progress in research, the future for the young exceptional child is full of promise.

Ponder These

1

Suppose you suspect that a child in your preschool group has a language deficiency. What would be the advantages and disadvantages of alerting the child's parents to his possible difficulty?

2

A six-year-old child with whom you work exhibits the following:

antisocial behavior (kicking, hitting, scratching, spitting on others)

severe language and speech disorders (poor articulation, poverty of expression)

lack of independent play skills (cannot play alone with toys)

lack of appropriate self-help skills (cannot feed himself without spilling or dress himself without help)

Which of the child's problem behaviors would you work on first? Why? How would you go about changing these behaviors?

3

Preschool teachers typically like to teach and want to teach children. But responsibilities and problems apart from teaching often compete for the teacher's time. List as many of these competing responsibilities and problems as you can. How could you structure the preschool day so that nonteaching responsibilities took less time?

References

Allen, K. E., J. Rieke, V. Dmitriev, and A. H. Hayden. Early warning: observation as a tool for recognizing potential handicaps in young children. *Educational Horizons,* 1972, *50,* 43–55.

Baldwin, A. L. (Ed.) *Theories of child development.* New York: Wiley, 1967.

Baratz, J. Linguistic and cultural factors in teaching reading to ghetto children. *Elementary English,* 1969, *46,* 199–203.

Bereiter, C. and S. Engelmann. *Teaching disadvantaged children in the preschool.* Englewood Cliffs, N.J.: Prentice-Hall, 1966.

Bloom, B. S. *Stability and change in human characteristics.* New York: Wiley, 1964.

Bloom, B., A. Davis, and R. Hess. *Compensatory education for cultural deprivation.* New York: Holt, Rinehart & Winston, 1965.

Caldwell, B. M. Consolidating our gains in early childhood. *Educational Horizons,* 1972, *50,* 56–62.

Evans, E. D. *Contemporary influences in early childhood education.* New York: Holt, Rinehart & Winston, 1971.

Grotberg, E. H. Review of research 1965 to 1969. Washington, D.C.: Project Head Start, Office of Economic Opportunity, 1969.

Hess, R. D. and V. Shipman. Cognitive elements in maternal behavior. In *The craft of teaching and the schooling of teachers.* Denver: U.S. Office of Education, Tri-University Project, 1967, 57–85.

Payne, J. S., C. D. Mercer, R. A. Payne, and R. G. Davison. *Head Start: A tragicomedy with epilogue.* New York: Behavioral Publications, 1973.

Piaget, J. *The origins of intelligence in children.* New York: International Universities, 1952.

Skeels, H. M. Adult status of children with contrasting early life experiences: a follow-up study. *Monographs of the Society for Research in Child Development,* 1966, *31,* No. 3 (Whole No. 105), 1–68.

Skinner, B. F. *Science and human behavior.* New York: Free Press, 1953.

Wallace, G. and J. M. Kauffman. *Teaching children with learning problems.* Columbus, Ohio: Charles E. Merrill, 1973.

ten

Conclusion

You should be somewhat aware by now of how we feel about handicapped children and of what it is like to teach them. We have provided some basic information concerning the definition, prevalance, and etiology of several handicapping conditions: learning disability, emotional disturbance, mental retardation, speech and language disorders, visual impairment, and hearing impairment. We have provided similar information on handicapping conditions in early childhood and on the nonhandicapping exceptionality of giftedness. We hope that you have also gained some knowledge of and feel for such essential concepts and crucial issues as labeling, psychoeducational versus behavioral techniques of behavior management, adult expectations for the retarded, stuttering, day schools versus institutional school programs for the blind, oral versus manual communication for the deaf, early identification of handicapping conditions, and differential education for the gifted.

But there is a lot left to say about exceptional children and their education. In particular, there are the facts about how these children and their parents get or do not get appropriate services.

Remember John, the emotionally disturbed child described in Chapter 3 — the one who really got the idea about the consequences

126

of his own behavior? Well, we did not tell you the whole story back there.

◦━◦

John was always a difficult child. His mother, an alcoholic, was at her wit's end to know how to manage him long before he was old enough to go to school. She blamed a lot of John's trouble on her husband, also an alcoholic, who was not at home much of the time and who was abusive when he was home. John's first-grade teacher complained that he was slow — immature, not "ready" for school or reading. But she did not have any helpful suggestions, except to just settle down and wait for him to get ready.

When John was in the second grade his family moved into a school district with a special education program. The school psychologist tested him early in the school year and reported that John was mildly retarded — IQ 68 — and ought to be in a special class for educable mentally retarded children. Because John's mother could not accept the idea of having a retarded child, she did not consent to having him placed in the special class. Meanwhile, John was not learning anything in school and his behavior was becoming more of a problem. The teacher was getting angry at having to put up with his constant running around the room, making noise, and getting into fights. Finally, under duress, John's mother gave the O.K. for him to be placed in the mentally retarded class.

It was in that class that John really started to kick up a fuss. He had tantrums, tore up his work, and would not obey the teacher. The school psychologist suggested to John's mother that she get some help for him, but failed to specify what kind or where. It turned out that the school psychologist was not really a psychologist at all, just someone with a degree in counseling who gave tests that he had not been trained to give or interpret. The mother also discovered that John's teacher had not been trained in special education, but was just a "mature" teacher who was not wanted for any other job.

What to do? Moving to another school district with better special education seemed to be the only solution.

John was tested by the school psychologist in the new district and came up with an IQ of 89 — he was not retarded, so he could not be in special education. Back in the regular class, however, John was a misfit. Not only was he surly, disobedient, and slow-learning, but the teacher noticed that he was awkward, clumsy, and "hyperactive." The teacher had the psychologist do some more testing. This time the psychologist said he found evidence of perceptual problems and brain damage and he referred John's mother to a pediatrician. The pediatrician in turn referred John's mother to a child neurologist, after telling her that he thought John might, in fact, be hyperactive and brain damaged. The child neurologist said that, yes, John probably was brain damaged and then prescribed some drugs. But things did not change at school.

At midyear the school district started a new special class for brain-damaged children. Most of these children were physically handicapped due to obvious brain damage and once again, John did not fit in very well. Neither did he like being transported clear across the county to a new class. The teacher said he was unmanageable. She thought he ought to be retested — maybe he was emotionally disturbed.

This time John was evaluated at the state psychiatric hospital. Results: low IQ, possible brain damage, and serious emotional disturbance. He ought to be institutionalized, they said, but there was a two-year waiting list.

So back to the brain-damaged class. John beat up one classmate on the bus and hit another one with a piece of chain he carried. Because the teacher was terrified, the school authorities decided that John should stay home for the rest of the year.

The next fall there was a new class for emotionally disturbed children — mine. John came to my class but remained on the waiting list at the state hospital. After four months in my class things seemed to be going along pretty well. Finally, John was learning, liked school, didn't cause too much trouble, and his mother was satisfied with his progress.

In the fifth month I received a call from a social worker at the state hospital. There was an unexpected opening for John. He would be admitted the following week.

An atypical case? No! It is not unusual for an exceptional child to be diagnosed and rediagnosed, referred and re-referred, labeled and relabeled. Unfortunately, even after parents and children are led through the thicket of clinical speculation, only approximately fifty per cent of those diagnosed receive special services. Finally, of those children who do receive services, many are bandied from one class or program to another. Exceptional children are too good to be treated this way.